BEAT COP CHICAGO BLUE: RECOLLECTIONS OF A "STREET GRUNT"

Book Two

Ben Celano

ISBN: 1546603859
ISBN 13: 9781546603856

DEDICATION

In my first book, I thought I could add a dedication after the book was completed. I was wrong. So, I will not make that mistake this time. During my police career, I worked with so many great people. I thank them for putting up with me, especially when I was "Joe New Guy." When you are new, your mistakes and missteps are legion. Most of the guys I worked with patiently put up with me until I found my legs. I thank my instructors at the police academy, for whom training my class must have seemed like herding cats. I thank my field training officers who tried to add to the foundation I received in the police academy. When I look back at the patience they had, I am truly grateful. Most of all, I thank all my partners over the years. They had my back when we were down in the blood and the mud. They are my brothers and sisters all. Our bonds will survive until death. I am sure I am alive today because of them. Some of the accounts in the first and second books are theirs as well as my own. We all have stories to tell. I hope I did them justice. My thanks to all the good sergeants, lieutenants, captains, and commanders who made our difficult work bearable by good counsel in times of need. The good bosses made you feel their supervision was not needed except for a little tweak here and there. It was a talent not all possessed.

*Thanks also to all the great detectives I worked with. Their help
was invaluable when navigating the criminal justice system. In
that same vein, I want to thank all the district tactical officers
who were there for me whenever I called for an assist.
Thanks also to my wife, family members, and friends who supported me
in the writing of books one and two. A special shout-out to my cousin
Agnes, who as a college instructor gave me invaluable advice on grammar
and punctuation. All of their support, was and is much appreciated.
I also want to thank my faithful dogs, past and present. They
were at my side through it all. To appropriate a saying horse-
lovers use and apply it to canines. "There is nothing so
good for the inside of a man as the outside of a dog."
I hope I am able to give the people who read this book a sense of what
we police officers all do every day. We do it so you do not have to.
Last on this page but first in my heart, I wish to salute the fallen,
the brave officers who gave their lives for the safety of strangers. I also
salute their wounded brothers and sisters who suffer both physical
and mental wounds with courage and grace. Like the brave officers
in New York on 9/11, they ran toward the danger. They did not
cower or question. They did it because it's what we do—heroes all.*

TABLE OF CONTENTS

*Good people sleep peaceably in their beds
at night only because rough men stand
ready to do violence on their behalf.*
—George Orwell

PREFACE

If you have already read *Beat Cop, Chicago Blue, Book One*, you know what to expect. I will state for those readers who have not read the first book that this book is not for the squeamish or sensitive soul. It is not for children or most women. If you have a soft heart, some of the stories may be upsetting to you. Both books are what street cops face daily. Just when you thought things could not get weirder, they do. So, if you are ready…

Here we go….

NAKED PEOPLE

THE SHIT BISCUIT

My partner and I were working the third watch when we got a call of a domestic disturbance with the son. At the time, I was a field training officer (FTO). My task was to guide a P.P.O. (Probationary Police Officer) through a familiarization with the procedures to follow when responding to calls. Unfortunately for her this was one of her first calls.

We arrived at the dispatched location to find two severely shaken parents. They had found that "Sonny Boy" was abusing anabolic steroids. Being good, caring parents, they confronted Sonny Boy with what they had found. Sonny Boy went into a rage and started trashing the house. When the parents tried to stop him, he became even more threatening. He was experiencing what shrinks call a *mood disorder*. The layman calls it *'roid rage*. Many times, the overuse of illegal, nonprescription steroids leads to psychiatric problems. In Sonny Boy's case, it took a bizarre turn.

According to his parents, he locked himself in the bathroom. After a while, he came out. He was naked. He also had smeared his own feces all over his body. Mom and Dad were terrified. It probably was not their proudest parental moment.

We put out a lookout on Sonny Boy on our way to start a search for this goof. It was a short description. Not many guys were walking around the 'hood naked and smeared with shit. We did not have to go very far. At the corner of the block was Sonny Boy in all his scatological glory. When we confronted Sonny Boy, we noticed he was growling, snorting, and drooling. Yippee.

I was pondering why the department had not issued us nets and tranquilizer-dart guns. I felt bad for my recruit, as I am sure she had never seen a snarling naked man covered in shit. Welcome to police work. It really is not as glamorous as it is portrayed on most of the TV programs. Most of your TV heroes are never going to tackle a naked, shit-covered man. Alas, it was our assignment.

There was plenty of help on the scene if we needed it. The other officers were also there to laugh their asses off. Laughing at other people's self-induced maladies was a perk that livened up our shift work. Laughing at your fellow police officer's plight was also a plus. It was like seeing a burglar stuck in the exhaust vent of a restaurant as the cook fires up the grill. Great fun.

The Chicago Fire Department (CFD) ambulance crew was there to see the fun too. The back doors of the ambulance were open, and the two EMTs were sitting on the bumper with a ringside seat. I am sure if someone had been selling popcorn, they would have done a brisk business.

We tried to talk to gurgling, snarling Sonny Boy, but to no avail. In whatever world he was in, being shit covered and naked was the way to be. We donned our Nitrile gloves. We approached Sonny Boy. He went into a crouch with his hands held in front of his body like claws. I think I was more afraid of this fuck biting me than I was of grappling with his feces-smeared self. When we got close, Sonny Boy collapsed onto the lawn and started to blubber and cry. We were able to cuff him without a struggle. Thank you, Jesus.

The other police officers present let out a collective groan of disappointment. I smiled like a crocodile. Spoiling others' fun is also fun. The CFD guys were also disappointed because now they had to care for Sonny Boy. That must have been most unpleasant. They headed to the hospital, where there was no shortage of crazies in the emergency room. We helped to strap Sonny Boy to a gurney. I soaked my handcuffs in some sort of green hospital liquid to kill any shit microbes.

We had already notified Sonny Boy's parents, who were destined to spend some time in a Chicago ER, for which they would probably need psychiatric help. It was like putting goats in a tiger pen—never a good mix. After completing all our reports, we relaxed a little in the hospital's police room. My recruit looked like she was wondering why she wanted this job. I told her not to worry, that there was worse yet to come. More fun. When she went home at night, she would be a little less normal than she was the night before. Her circle of civilian friends would shrink. Almost all the people who would understand her would be other coppers. Welcome to the brotherhood, sister.

THE TRAFFIC CONE

It was about noon on a pretty nice day. I was patrolling an area known for rampant drug activity, plus the daily shootings that accompanied that trade. Come to think of it, there weren't many places in the district that didn't qualify for that description.

There was a slow-moving car to my front. I dropped back a little in case I needed room to maneuver. I was already moving at a fairly slow pace when the car to my front came to a complete stop. I got ready to exit my vehicle quickly. I jammed it in park, unsnapped my holster, and then pushed my door open.

A heavyset man in his forties got out of the vehicle. He never looked at me. He started walking away from me. I got on the radio and told dispatch my location and situation. I ran the plate to see if it was a stolen car or if the occupant was wanted. As I was doing this, I was trying to stop the man walking away from me. I yelled for him to stop, but he kept walking. Then, to my surprise, he started to take his clothing off. First came the shirt. He continued walking. Then off came the pants. Now I did not want to catch up to him.

I called for an ambulance. My guess was that he was on PCP. Many times, people on PCP will take off their clothes because they feel uncomfortably hot. PCP is also a hallucinogen. So, his reality was different from mine. He may have thought he was at Disneyland. Come to think of it, so did I. PCP also is a pain killer, so pain compliance was not going to be effective. Now off came the shorts. Yikes.

At this point, there would be no grappling if it could be avoided. He was headed for a major four-lane commercial street. He took off his shoes and socks as he reached the road. I caught up to him. I stopped traffic just as he began to walk across the street. When he got halfway across, he turned ninety degrees and sat down. He was an ample man of about 260 pounds. One ass cheek was on one side of the double line that ran down the middle of the street, and the other ass cheek was equally apportioned. His eyes were staring straight ahead as he piloted the Millennium Falcon through deep space.

When the ambulance got there, we managed to get Hans Solo into it. Soon he was on his way to meet Luke Skywalker in the ER of the local hospital. I walked back to my squad car, picking up his shoes and outer clothing. His socks and underwear would remain where they fell. The local rats could use them for bedding. I pulled his car to the side of the road; he had left the keys in the vehicle. I headed to the hospital to do the paperwork. Just another day on the planet Endor.

THE BEAN BAG

My partner and I rolled up on a street disturbance just after midnight. There was a good-sized crowd in the street. There were a lot of shirtless, sweaty young men running around with baseball bats, wooden sticks, and primitive weapons of various types. It was midnight, it was hot, and there was mob of armed people in the street. What could go wrong?

We called in an "on-view" disturbance, then asked for an assist car to start rolling our way. We cautiously got out of the car to see what was going on. We stopped one of the sweaty young men carrying a baseball bat. He dropped the bat as our hands went to our holsters. A bat can kill you just as dead as a .45-caliber slug.

He pointed down the street. Of course, the neighborhood yahoos had broken the streetlight, so we had a hard time seeing what was happening. The sweaty young man told us that a rapist had been threatening the neighborhood women. The men were taking care of business. Some street justice was being meted out to the rapist.

We put his bat in the trunk of our car, then began walking toward the fur ball farther down the street. As we approached, some of the street-justice vigilantes started to melt away. When we were finally close enough to see what was going on, we spied a large, naked, bleeding man.

He was perhaps six foot four and about 280 pounds. Any physically lesser man probably would have died from the beating he received. We immediately called for an ambulance. This guy was really hurt by the street mob. He was bruised and bleeding all over. We asked some of the crowd what had happened. After sorting through all the bullshit, we ascertained that apparently the man had overdosed on PCP. As with most PCP, users he took off his clothes. He started wandering the neighborhood. Some woman freaked out when she saw him and screamed. In the "telephone game" of the 'hood, that scream turned into a rape.

All the young thugs in the 'hood took offense to the man's alleged offense. These are the same thugs who slap their girlfriends around daily, by the way, but this for them was too much to bear. With any excuse for violence, as was their mantra, they brutally attacked the drug-addled man. We eventually got him into an ambulance. We had no witnesses to the battery of the man. Our victim could not help us because he was for the time being in an alternate reality. As we headed to the hospital to do our report, we both knew this guy was going to come off his high in a world of hurt.

THE DANCING MACHINE

We got a call of a disturbance with a "mental." We rolled up to the address just as a couple more cars pulled up. They were volunteer back-ups. You never knew with a mental which way shit was going to jump. It never hurt to have too many coppers than too few. Sometimes things went smooth as silk, sometimes not.

God seems to have given people with mental problems compensating muscle mass and strength. A mentally disturbed person could be very dangerous. As it turned out, the mental was a young lady. In all other respects, she looked normal. What was not normal was that she was dancing about like a ballerina and was taking off her clothing. She smiled at us. We smiled back. We tried talking to her, but we might as well have been talking to the moon. We were about to see the moon.

She went into a break-dance move. Her legs were up in the air and she was twirling on her back. The uncovered moon was in full view along with several other feminine parts. We stood there a moment, open mouthed. She would have made Beyonce envious.

At last we had to act, but grabbing a naked dancing woman was not something most of us did on a regular basis. First, we stopped the spinning by grabbing her legs. Then we managed to flip her over to be cuffed. Next, we tried to drape some of her clothing over her. We were partially successful.

She giggled and giggled all the way down the stairs. We managed to get her in a wagon without much trouble except for the leering crowd outside of the building. She was on her way to the hospital for some medication. All of the police officers at the scene were smiling, a very rare thing. God had given us a task that was not unpleasant. Thank you, God of Naked Dancing Women. We are but servants in your army.

SNICKERS

"Snickers" had been his nickname since he was a wee tyke. Why Snickers? His family and friends would tell you it was because he was a little bit nuts. As he grew, he amplified his reputation by committing numerous acts of moronic brutality. He was someone you did not want to cross. He did not belong to a gang, although he had a gang member's common trait of stultifying stupidity. He also had an amazing athletic ability, as we later found out.

On this particular day, he had shot an individual who had run afoul of his temper. The victim was another example of the cretinous genus to which Snickers belonged. But alas, that victim would live and breed thanks to excellent emergency room doctors and nurses. Our task was to round up Snickers and bring him before the bar. However, finding a jury of his peers might be difficult.

That said, we set out to find him. He was last seen near one of our expressways with no shirt on. Some veteran officers who had dealt with Snickers through the years started heading to where he stayed. He still lived with his mom and dad, who defended him as if he were the second coming.

One of the guys spotted him near a large public park. The chase was on. Cars swarmed the area. We alerted the adjoining suburbs. Some of their cars joined us in the search. We were about two miles from Snickers's home. Most fleeing subjects, like a rabbit, run a short distance, stop, and then hide. Searching them out is not easy. The number of multiunit apartment buildings, abandoned homes, alleys, and lots strewn with abandoned autos gave a fleet-footed subject plenty of opportunities for concealment.

Snickers, however, was on the move. He was spotted again, now wearing a shirt. He had probably clipped a shirt off someone's clothesline or taken it off someone's back. Although Snickers was not book smart, he had from years of criminal activity developed a cunning that served him well in defeating our efforts to capture him. He was spotted again, still on the move. He was running full out diagonally from the crime scene toward his home. He had already covered a mile at Olympic speed.

The officers staked out near his home waited patiently for him to appear. We continued the pursuit like hounds after a fox. He must have thought we did not know who he was because he was still charting his course toward Mom and Dad. If asked, we were sure Mom and Dad would vouch that he had been home asleep when the shooting took place. Mom and Dad were no fans of the police. The veteran officers who had staked out Snickers's home were rewarded when he appeared running down the block. He had run more than two miles through yards and alleys in less than fifteen minutes. He had dumped the gun probably in the park's lagoon where it would never be found.

The stakeout officers radioed that they had Snickers in sight. But, like the savvy criminal he was, he entered another home. We found out it was his auntie's house, though possibly it was his play auntie. The stakeout crew followed him up the stairs into the house, and he was taken into custody. A small crowd had gathered outside. It was evening, it was hot, and there were numerous police vehicles in the street—a surefire recipe for unrest.

Many of the residents, if asked one on one, appreciate the police patrolling their neighborhoods. However, when in a crowd, some had to demonstrate their anger at the "man." Hating on the police bolstered their street cred'. Never mind that Snickers had just shot a man. It was a "fuck the police" moment. Yippee.

It seems odd to those of us who enforce the laws of the people's elected representatives that when people are shot or killed, it is trumpeted that the police are not doing their job. However, when we apprehend the criminal, such as Snickers, it is part of a master plan of mass incarceration fomented by the prison/industrial complex. Total horse shit.

Finally, the arresting officers came out with Snickers handcuffed. They were walking him down the stairs, and Snickers seemed cooperative. The officers, who were trying to make sure they did not fall down the stairs, unfortunately did not have an iron grip on Snickers. Snickers tugged away from the officer's grip. Then I witnessed his athletic ability first hand. He did a back flip over the banister. He stuck the landing a la Nadia Comaneci. He took off at a dead run with all of us in pursuit.

At the back of the property was a six-foot cyclone fence. I thought, "We got him." I was wrong. Snickers, at a full-out run with handcuffs on, high-jumped the fence. All the coppers in the yard could not believe what they had just seen. Everybody just said, "Fuck." Some guys headed for their cars. Some were jumping fences in adjoining yards heading for the alley. He was gone. We searched for more than an hour but never found him.

For the next three days, we showed up at his house at all hours to see if he had come home. His mother and father got real sick of seeing us at their door. Finally, after three days, he showed up at the station with Mom and Dad. The case went nowhere, after all that work. The thug he shot refused to cooperate. A mountain of paperwork for nothing.

The officers who caught Snickers had disciplinary procedures instituted against them for letting a prisoner escape. Sometimes we lose one. Sometimes a policeman's life is not a happy one. Shit happens. Sometimes it happens to you.

A few years later someone told me Snickers had caught a bullet in the bean. His luck had run out. The "payback bitch" had come for Snickers.

<u>JASPER</u>

Jasper was like a fixture on the street. He was a panhandler. It was his spot. After a while you barely noticed him. He was about fifty years old, as scruffy as can be, and had an unkempt beard, which we figured must have been infested with a variety of beard vermin. He wore an old, greasy winter hat with flaps no matter the season. A bulky three-quarter-length coat covered his flannel shirt and bib overalls. His footwear was a pair of old galoshes over some sport shoes. He looked like he needed the money. His methodology was to stand in the median of a major avenue with an old plastic soda cup, which he rattled at motorists who had stopped at the traffic light.

We mostly left him alone because he smelled like urine and fecal matter seasoned with a touch of ammonia. His off-putting odor made your eyes water. This, we later learned, was a tactic to keep the police at bay. His odor was like porcupine quills; you just wanted to leave him be. But, a fly was about to land in my bowl of soup.

Jasper, as I mentioned, was on a main avenue, which ran under a major expressway. Jasper's spot was also at the exit ramp from the expressway. On that particular beat, there were some factories that had been there since World War II. The factories were now abandoned and were in the process of being demolished. A new business that made movies had moved in.

The moviemakers were good businesspeople who brought jobs to the city. They made movies in a number of Chicago locations, including the area now occupied by the movie studio. That gave them "clout." Jasper had no "clout." Jasper's problem was about to involve the movie industry. It was also going to start a major crap boulder streaking toward me like a Tomahawk cruise missile.

I got called in to the district one fine day. I was told in no uncertain terms that Jasper had to go. I inquired as to the reason and was told that some Hollywood star had expressed his distaste for Jasper's presence and appearance. A call was made to city hall where the "Anointed One" ruled. The Anointed One called his appointed ones. The appointed ones called the unappointed ones. The unappointed ones called in the unwilling one. Me.

The crap boulder was rolling. Tasked with this unpleasant duty, I felt that I might as well get it over with—the sooner the better. I found Jasper and told him he would have to relocate because we were getting complaints about him. He readily agreed, picked up his water bottle with some other paraphernalia, and walked toward the underpass nearby. The underpass held a "*Star Wars* bar" collection of characters who lived under the bridge. I thought, "Well, problem solved."

Three hours later as I was on my way to another job, I passed Jasper's spot. He had returned. Before I could get back to him, another call was placed to the mayor's office complaining about our lack of action on this pressing crime problem. I was called in again and was told to solve this problem by a very unhappy watch commander who had had his rear end blistered by his overlords. The crap boulder was getting more localized.

This time when I went to Jasper's spot, I put him in the car. It was a very unpleasant act. I drove him to another spot where he could run his hustle without offending the Hollywood elite's sensibilities. What I did not know was that the new spot was another panhandler's spot. In the world of "Panhandlerdom," taking another's spot was a definite violation of the "panhandler's code of conduct." Jasper's counterpart opened up a can of panhandler whup ass on him. The next day, Jasper was back at his old spot with a mark or two.

Another call was made. Splat. The crap boulder landed on me. I was told to do what I had to do, absent murder, to solve this problem. At this point, I had no other option but to arrest Jasper. Jasper had been violating a city ordinance. It was an ordinance not usually enforced, but desperate times demanded desperate measures.

Jasper was very unhappy with my decision, but he did not give me any trouble. Since he was in custody, I had to do a custodial search. It was a most unpleasant task. As I mentioned, Jasper used his revolting stench as a defense against arrest.

When I brought him into the district, the desk mice were smirking with joy at a fellow officer's discomfort. I felt that natural animosity of a working policeman toward the people whose biggest decision of the day was what they were going to eat for free. I wrote up Jasper and took him to the lockup, where I got another ration of shit for bringing the lockup guys their own personal porcupine. They had to search then print the odiferous Jasper. I felt their pain. They too were the working police.

I cleaned up. I was ready to hit the street when the lockup keeper tracked me down. First, he told me that Jasper's one phone call was to a girlfriend. We marveled at the fact that he was some woman's bearded Lothario. Also, he told me that Jasper had about ninety clams in his shoe. We talked a minute and came to the conclusion that Jasper was taking down about $70K a year tax free. Hmm. We laughed. We vowed upon retiring that we would grow scruffy beards and buy plastic cups. We would live the dream. We laughed. The desk mice frowned at our joy.

When the movie was over, Jasper got his spot back. Nobody ever bothered him again.

THE TWO JUDYS

JUDY I

Judy was on the near side of seventy-five. She was short, more from age than heredity. The first time I ran into her was while I was on foot patrol. She always had something interesting to say. The problem is that when you grow old, people stop listening. You become kind of invisible. Her language was a tad rougher than my basic training drill sergeant. She had, after all, grown up during the Great Depression. She had seen World War II, Korea, and Vietnam. She had seen the "can do" attitude of America turn into the "won't do" attitude of the 1960s to the "what can you do for me" attitude of the 1990s.

She had been around the block a couple times. She let you know she was nobody's patsy. But, as I said, nobody wanted to listen to some "old broad," as she called herself. When you're old, you cannot hear or see as well. You walk a little slower when you amble into the next room, and then forget why you are there. As I see it, wisdom is the sum of both good and bad life experiences.

Judy had wisdom in spades, as do most people who have lived a long life. But, as with most people her age, nobody asks what you think about anything. To others, you are too old, so how could you possibly know anything?

This was Judy. She had nobody except a cat. There was a daughter that came to visit once in a while, but like most modern families, her daughter had her own life to deal with. Many years ago, extended family members lived in the same house or nearby. In some families, a son or daughter would stay with mom until the end. They would forego marriage to take care of mom.

It was a different world that Judy would die in. Judy would tell me about her old beaus. She claimed one still pursued her. She showed me pictures from when she had been a young lass. She had been a real looker. She told me she had been a stripper for a while after the war.

Time had a way of unkindly taking one's youth. It slowly made you pay for any youthful indiscretions. If you smoked, it took your breath. If you drank, it took your liver. If you ate to the point of obesity, diabetes might lay you low. We are all on the same road. Some of us will get off sooner, and some later.

Judy seemed to be pretty tough. She would give the reaper a fight. One very hot day, it was in the upper nineties, and I saw Judy walking down the street about a half mile from her apartment. When you are seventy-five and it is ninety-seven degrees, you are rolling the dice with the reaper.

I recalled a weekend in July 1995 when it was 105 degrees. Fortunately for me, I was out of town. The police department and the medical examiner's office were overwhelmed. Almost 750 people died. Most of them were elderly people with no air conditioners or fans. Judy survived that one. Since then, when the weather was dangerously hot, the city checked the voting rolls for the elderly, and the police department tried to contact everyone older than sixty-five. If they could not be reached by phone, the beat cops were given a list of people to contact. We went to seniors' homes to check if they were OK. Some public buildings were opened as cooling centers, including the police stations. Although our station had only a few air conditioners, it was better than nothing at all. Some businesses and charities contributed electric fans for the seniors.

When I saw Judy, she was on her way to get a fan. However, the church that was distributing them was three miles from her apartment. Not only was it three miles to the church but it was through some of the roughest streets on the west side. Most of the gang thugs would not bother an elderly person, but some drug-using hypes would. The bottom line was that even as gritty as Judy was, she could not carry a large window fan three miles back home in ninety-seven-degree heat.

I stopped Judy and told her to jump in the beat car. I drove her to the church and then back to her home. A few months later, Judy's daughter sought me out. Judy had passed in her sleep. She died alone except for the cat.

Judy's daughter thanked me for looking out for her mom. For me, it would be a little sadder world without her squeaky voice and salty talk. I missed seeing her.

Judy was a little bit of joy in many otherwise crappy days.

JUDY II

I was rolling down one of the main drags at patrol speed. Patrol speed was between five and fifteen miles per hour. At this speed, you could see into stores, check parked cars for meter violations, and make sure the ne'er-do-wells weren't ne'er-do-welling.

Because of my speed, I was waving cars behind me to pass. Soon, I noticed traffic was still backing up even though the traffic light was green. I heard some screeching brakes and horns blowing. When I was finally able to ascertain the cause of the traffic slowdown, I was a little surprised but not surprised. Usually, these kinds of problems occurred during the evening hours.

Three young ladies were walking down the boulevard. Like the "Big Bopper" said, they had a little "wiggle in their walk." This was causing a "gapers' block." I thought, "I must talk to these ladies regarding their causing a traffic backup." They dissolved into the corner liquor store. I parked my patrol car.

As I entered the liquor store, all three young ladies were at the counter. I tapped the shoulder of the girl with the most outrageous *bootyous maximus*. She turned and I saw that she was just as outrageous in the bow as she was at the stern. She had the face of an angel. I told her that she and her friends had snarled traffic for blocks. She smiled, revealing that she had five front teeth missing. She laughed. I thought irreverent cop thoughts to myself. Either she was doing meth and had meth mouth (where the gums get spongy and the teeth fall out), or her pimp was knocking her around.

All three girls were prostitutes. Judy was in the 'hood visiting her sisters, whom I knew. They were also prostitutes. They were living nearby with their burglar man friends. Those guys were a two-man crime wave. The girls tricked and the burglars burgled, all to get high. They were doing heroin and coke and injected both to intensify the high and mitigate the negatives of both drugs.

The trouble with speedballing is that you can stop breathing, a la John Belushi. Death is Mother Nature's way of telling you to slow down. In the end, the girls and I exchanged pleasantries. I warned them not to work my patch. We parted as friends. About a year later, Judy was found in a boxcar cut up with a razor. Her pimp went for the murder.

WELCOME TO THE NEIGHBORHOOD I

M ister Cirillo was one of the greatest generation. As a young man, he had stormed through Europe and fought Adolph Hitler's SS in the Battle of the Bulge. He had crossed the Rhine. He had been wounded and come home. He was part of the nine million American men under arms who swept across North Africa, Sicily, Italy, France, Germany, and the numerous islands of the Pacific. They gave their youth and blood to free mankind from the terrible yoke of dictators who endeavored to enslave or exterminate the peoples of the world.

Mister Cirillo had recovered from his wounds, got a job, married, raised a family, and worked to make a life for himself and his family. Now he was older and had retired. The kids were gone and married. It was just he and his wife. She had recently taken ill, so he looked after her day and night; he fed her, washed her, and clothed her.

I first ran into him while on foot patrol. He was tending some flowers in front of the apartment building in which he lived. I stopped, we chatted, and we became friends. When you shook his hand, you knew you were shaking hands with a man. He also had a wonderful smile and a great sense of humor. I met his wife one day as they came home from the doctor. She was also a sweet, wonderful person. He had to help her from the car and up the stairs.

As time went on, dementia took hold of his wife. She became less mobile. He had to carry her if she needed to use the bathroom or clean up when it was too late. Being a caregiver became more difficult as time went by. Mister Cirillo's love for his wife was a constant. He lived life as it should be lived.

Enter the "Shitbird brothers," "Snoopy" and "Stubby." My first encounter with them was about a week after they moved into their mother's small apartment. The brothers were in their middle twenties. They had no jobs and were sponging off Mom. As I found out later, both had done time for robbery.

One day, an elderly lady was playing a poker machine in one of the businesses on the strip. She was playing for recreation only, to be sure. She felt someone's hand in her pocket. It was Snoopy Shitbird. She told me about it, and I paid a visit to the Shitbirds' apartment. The lady did not wish to pursue the matter, but I warned the Shitbirds that they were now on my radar. Strike one.

On another occasion, I stopped them with a shopping bag full of meat. These nitwits didn't have an honest nickel between them. They had no receipt. I went with them to talk to Mama Shitbird. She disavowed her progeny. I called the store, and indeed, the meat had been lifted from there. The store, however, did not wish to pursue it. They would write it off. Strike two.

So, the Shitbirds skated again. When I could, after roll call, I would stop by the review office to check out the case reports from the previous day. I saw Mr. Cirillo's name; he had been robbed.

Two men had accosted him in the alley as he parked in his garage. They tried to grab his wife's purse. When he tried to stop them, he was struck. They took what money the couple had.

When I talked to Mr. Cirillo, he told me his wife was still frightened. If you think that my first thought after reading the report was of the Shitbird brothers, you are dead on. The descriptions fit them like the peel on a banana. In the following days, there were two more robberies. Same description.

In the meantime, I ran the brothers for an I.R.(identification records) number and photos. Their rappers came back with thefts and robberies. I alerted some guys I knew on the tactical team, and they did the legwork with the photos. They got two IDs on one brother and one possible on the other. Usually, one was a lookout while the other committed the robbery. They were both arrested. Strike three.

One of the brothers was ID'd in a lineup. He went for two of the robberies. The other Shitbird Brother was not identified. He skated again. Not long after, what was left of the Shitbird family moved away.

Mr. Cirillo's wife never got over her fright. She crossed over a few months later. Afterward, I would see Mr. Cirillo tending his flowers. We would talk, but I could tell the joy had gone from his life. About a year later, he joined his wife. He was a good man. God bless. If there is a heaven, he is in it.

I hope, for justice's sake, when the Shitbird brothers breathe their last, that Mr. Cirillo is the angel tasked with leading them to the lower regions to serve their time. I think they will arrive limping and with a few less teeth.

THE CONS

When I say *cons* in the following vignettes, I do not mean convicts; I mean the schemes that confidence men run. They are called *confidence men* because they are so proficient at gaining your trust or confidence. Many times, even the people cheated cannot believe they have been cheated. That is how good they are.

Con men come in all shapes and sizes. They afflict every strata of society. The people conned by Bernie Madoff for millions could not believe they had been hustled. They were rich, intelligent, and accomplished people. They fell for the oldest scam in the book, the Ponzi scheme. They believed that they were so much smarter because the paper profits they were making were so much higher than everyone else's. If they wanted their money, Bernie would pay them with another sucker's money.

P. T. Barnum had it right: "There's a sucker born every minute." The second part of that old saw is, "And there is a hustler born every hour to trim 'em." Most of the con men or women are real lowlifes.

Many of the people they cheat are the elderly. The elderly, as we know, grew up in a different era. They didn't lock their doors. Kids came home when the streetlights came on. Neighbor helped neighbor. Those times are gone, and things have changed for the worse. The bottom line is that most people raised in those times had a high level of trust for their fellow man. Also, they find it embarrassing to admit they have been fooled. That's human nature. Below are some incidents that are typical in today's world.

⊸⊹⊱

A young man showed up at a woman's door claiming to be a handyman. He asked if there was anything to be done in her home. She was in her declining years, and her husband had passed. Problems that her husband used to take care of were piling up. Dripping faucets, a running toilet, squeaky doors, and dirty windows were some things she could no longer cope with.

The young man said he would do any work for very little money and a sandwich. She invited him in. He looked the house over on the inside, then on the outside. He told her he discovered several issues with the outside siding. It would require some patching and painting. He said he had to measure the house to see how much paint he would need. He asked her to stand by the back door and hold one end of a string he would use to measure the house. She held the string as he unrolled it from a ball and walked toward the front of the house. She held it for quite a while and didn't know that the young man had tied it to a lamp.

In the hallway, the woman had hung a sheet to eliminate drafts and keep the heat in the rear of the house. The sheet also blocked her view of the young man as he rifled through her jewelry and took cash from a purse hung on a doorknob. Then he was gone. She had been conned.

⊶ ⊷

A ninety-year-old woman lived with her eighty-eight-year-old sister. Her sister was not very mobile, so the ninety-year-old had to do most of the daily chores: the cooking, dish washing, laundry, dusting, plus all the unseen things that keep a house clean and running smoothly—all was done by the older sister. She had a son who checked on her and his aunt, but he lived some distance away. She also did the shopping for her and her sister. She would walk ten city blocks to the grocery store with a grocery cart. Ten city blocks is a little more than a mile. Then she would walk back with the cart containing her purchases. This was quite a feat for someone of her age.

One day as she was coming out of the store, a man asked her for some money because he was hungry. She, being a lovely person, gave the man a few dollars. He told her he would pay her back. He asked for her address so he could repay her. She told him. That evening, there was a knock on the door. He was not there to pay her back but to ask for more money. He told her that he had had a phone call from a dying relative in another state. He needed the money to travel to see the relative.

She gave him all the money she had in the house, $100, as her sister chided her not to do it. I am sure some element of fear had now entered the equation. The man was out the door in a flash. The woman's kindness had made her a victim. She had been conned. As you can imagine, it could have been worse. I called her son, and he came immediately. He was very lucky his mother had not been harmed.

⊶ ⊷

An elderly lady answered her door. On her front porch were two women who claimed they were from the Cook County Agency for the Aged. They showed the lady their credentials. She asked them to come in. They told her they wanted to interview her about her health and well-being. They sat.

After a while, one lady asked for a glass of water. When the woman got up, the other lady said, "Oh no, I will get it myself. Where is the kitchen?" When the woman came back from the kitchen, they quickly finished their interview and left. Several days later, the woman found the $200 she had placed between the pages of her Bible was gone. She had been conned.

Two elderly sisters lived together in a modest single-family home. They were both in their nineties. One sister enjoyed sitting in the front picture window. She could not walk very well. She loved to see what was going on in the neighborhood and would wave to people passing by.

One day a white van with several men inside passed by. She waved. They waved back. They stopped the van. They reversed and then pulled in the driveway. She had just waved to Gypsies.

Gypsies, or as they call themselves, *Romani*, are pros at fleecing the elderly. When the younger sister answered the door, one of the men said, "Excuse me, but do you have any pets or children here?" She answered that her grandson was there while his mother was at work. The man apologetically said that they had been working at her neighbor's home. He said that they had accidentally sprayed rat poison in her yard. He said he would show her where the poison was so she could keep her grandchild from the area.

She agreed to accompany him to the yard. As she left with him, another man appeared at the door. The sister from the window came into the kitchen. The second man told the sister to boil some water to pour on the rat poison. As she was struggling to find a pot, another man came in another unlocked door. He went directly to the bedrooms and went through drawers and purses.

The sister who had gone to the yard suddenly realized what was going on. She walked back to the house and told the men to get out. They did and left quickly. They got about $300 and some jewelry.

These kinds of scams are the Romani's specialty. They pose as workmen for the water department who are testing water. They pose as electrical workers who are checking circuit breakers. They pose as contractors inspecting siding and roof shingles they claim to have installed previously. The cons are limited only by the imagination and the gullibility of their elderly victims. This is how they live. I think there must be a special place in hell for the Romani. It is well deserved.

⊨⊨ ⊨⊨

A tragic event occurred involving a student at the local school. An eight-year-old had been accidentally shot. It seems her older brother was playing with a handgun. He pulled the trigger, killing his sister.

I knew her. She was a vivacious child with a wonderful smile. She would smile no more. Her laugh would be heard no more. I stopped at the school the morning after the news hit, and some of the staff were talking about the little girl.

I overheard one of the staff members who lived in the neighborhood comment that she had given ten dollars to the girl's family. I inquired to whom she had given the money. She replied that a man had come to her door with a clipboard containing a list of contributors who had given to the family. The story was that the girl's family did not have enough money to bury the little girl.

I told her she had been conned. She became angry with me. She protested and said that the man collecting the money was trying to help the girl's family. He had the newspaper article reporting her tragic death. On the clipboard was a list of contributors, and he penciled her name in with her contribution.

I asked the school secretary to find the phone number for the girl's family. I spoke with the child's mother and asked her if she had authorized anyone to collect money on her behalf. She said she had not. I thanked her. When I told the staff member of my inquiry, she became angrier with me. She walked away. I understood.

Most people who have been conned cannot believe it. I saddled up and tried to find the jackal who was sliming his way through the neighborhood, but he was gone. I got an assignment to see a lady about a theft. She lived not far from the school. She had been a victim of the same man who had conned the staff member and had given him eighty dollars. She was embarrassed. She was in her early seventies.

It seemed that I had to do something before he scammed the whole neighborhood, so I called a news radio station. Most of the older people still listened to the radio. I got lucky, and within an hour, it was being broadcast that a scam artist was taking advantage of the seniors in the neighborhood. Soon after, I was told to go in and see the DC (district commander).

He had received calls from three TV stations asking about the incidents. He was not angry or annoyed; he thought it was a good idea. He then explained to me the proper procedure to do what I had done. He also told me that reporters from the TV stations were on their way to interview me about the incident. I said I would prefer not to do the interviews, deferring to his greater media savvy. He laughed and told me that was not happening. He sent me down to wait for the reporters.

In the meantime, I started my case report. I managed to struggle through the TV interviews. One reporter followed me into the station from the interview; he wanted to interview the woman who had been scammed. I told him how embarrassed she was that she had been conned, but he kept at me about it. I gave him a definite "no." I was working on the report while talking to him, and he read my victim's name and address upside down from the report. That night I saw my victim on the news. The SOB went to her home and interviewed her even though I had asked him not to. Freedom of the press, I guess.

I called him the next day. I was pissed. He explained that he had not shown her face in the report. I said my piece and hung up on the weasel. In my opinion, she had been victimized twice. At least the scammer did not get any more money from the neighborhood.

They say these are not violent crimes. This is true; they do not involve physical violence. But the damage they do to people cannot be dismissed. It takes a dark soul to take money in these circumstances. None of these victims had very much money. They believed in the basic goodness of man. They wanted to help. In many cases, even if we collar the scum running the hustles, the victims are hesitant about coming forward. They are afraid of looking foolish.

I do not know if we can ever win this battle. Ever since that lady said, "Go ahead, take a bite of this apple," we as humans have been subject to being manipulated. I guess the answer is to trust no one.

My personal hope is that in the afterlife, as the con men approach the pearly gates, they have a conversation with Saint Peter, the keeper of the keys to paradise. He knows their pasts and posits a little con of his own. They are asked if they want to meet the "Morning Star," the "Shining One," the "Bringer of Light." They all assumed he's speaking of Jesus or God the Father. "Yes" is always the answer. The con is that the Morning Star happens to be that jolly fellow known as Lucifer, the Burning Beast of Hell. "What goes around comes around," sayeth the Lord. Amen.

THE SMASH-AND-GRAB
BROTHERS

In another scheme to terrorize elderly people, exclusively woman, shitbird criminals wait near a traffic light. They wait for elderly white women as the passsengers in a vehicle or a single-white woman, unaccompanied by a man to stop at the traffic signal.

If you ask why I am using race in this narrative, it is because black women are more aware of the criminal element seeking to take their money. They conceal their money and valuables so as not to have them taken from them. If you want to take a black woman's money or bling, you are in for a fight. They may not always win that fight, but you are not going to get away uninjured.

Most elderly white women passengers in a car have their purses in their lap. Most white woman drivers leave their purse on the passenger seat. They never anticipate that some shitbird is going to smash their passenger window sending shattered glass into their face then take their purse.

My partner and I responded to a smash and grab not far from the police station. At the scene, we found an elderly woman in shock. She had flecks of glass all over her face. She was bleeding where several shards had punctured her skin. She was the passenger in a car driven by her husband. My partner and I took the report. We called in the CFD to treat her injuries. We also tried to clean up all the shattered glass so that after a visit to the hospital they could safely drive their car home.

We were pissed. It was like seeing your grandmother white with shock, bleeding and frightened. We were going to find these guys. At our first opportunity, we hit the review office. We started going over all similar reports. With few exceptions, the reports highlighted similar descriptions, hours the crimes were committed, and the locations of the crimes. We came up with ten-plus strong-arm robberies by these same shitbirds.

We were looking for one, possibly two teens usually hitting on the weekends or in the evening hours in an eleven-block stretch of a main street running north to south. We thought that the weekend and evening hits were because they were probably in school during the day. We started doing a lot of street stops in the area of the robberies. Eventually, we came up with some names. It was two brothers. They were eleven and twelve years old. I'd had an encounter with them on a previous occasion when they had refused to get off a bus on which they had not paid the fare. That was settled by taking them off the bus. Now we had to find them.

We hit the schools in the area. I had the name of one of them from the bus incident; the other had run from that scene. There were six grammar schools in the area of the robberies. These mutts had a very common last name, so it took a little digging. We got lucky at the second school. We got their address, but when we went to it, the address was bogus. We asked people in the building if they knew the two little mopes.

They had stolen from most of the people in the building. The residents pointed us to an adjacent building. We went there and asked the people in the courtyard if they knew these guys. They pointed us to a second-floor apartment. We knocked on the door, and a small woman about thirty years old opened it. The hallway lights were all knocked out as they were in most of the buildings in this area.

We asked the woman if the two shitbirds lived there. She looked confused. At that point, we heard a door open toward the rear of the apartment. I stumbled toward the rear of the apartment. When I got to the rear landing, one of the brothers was already at the bottom of the stairs. I headed out after him. We were both running down an alley. He was twelve. I was forty-six. Needless to say, he won that foot race. Just as I almost caught up with him, he looked over his shoulder and laughed at me. He then turned on the afterburners and disappeared around a corner.

I walked back to the apartment where my partner had collared the other mope. It was as dark as a moonless night inside the apartment. The electricity had been cut off, and there was no food in the refrigerator or in the cabinets. There was also no furniture. The brothers had been sleeping on the floor. The mother appeared to have a diminished capacity.

We took our guy in and called the kiddie cops. We started calling previous victims for a lineup. We had four of the ten come in, and of those, only two ID'd our arrestee. While the juvenile officer was processing him, we shot back to the apartment. Laughing Boy had come back home. He tried the same trick, but I was waiting for him on the back stairs. Now I laughed. He also got ID'd. Bingo.

Normally, even though these idiots had committed multiple robberies, they would have been sent back home to their mama. Great system we got here. But the mother had to come in because they were juveniles, and she told the juvenile officer that she could not handle the boys. Her statement, coupled with the fact that there was no food, furniture, or electricity, got these guys shipped off to Maryville through Department of Children and Family Services (DCFS) intervention. Maryville was an institution for kids whose parents could no longer support them.

We cleared some robberies, and stopped others from happening. We felt pretty good. I ran into one of the brothers about six years later when I was bringing a prisoner back to the lockup. Laughing Boy was going for a burglary. I asked about his brother. He told me he was doing a dime for robbery. Some people may say that their poverty drove them to this life. I say you don't smash a car window in a grandmother's face because you are poor. Abe Lincoln was poor. You do that because you are evil.

IT'S YOUR TURN

W hen you are partners for a while, you become like brothers. Most times you spend more time with your partner
than you do your own family. You become close because your lives
depend upon each other. These are not just words—a bond de-
velops that will last a lifetime. You are both armed. You have the
power to take life in defense of others. You have the power to take
liberty if someone violates the legally binding norms of society that
we call laws. That is a lot of power and responsibility.

You have to know that when your back is turned to the bad guys
that your partner is looking out for you. He has your back, as the
saying goes. You start to know which way shit is going to jump by
your partner's words and mannerisms. But we would rather talk
than fight. We are not supermen; you cannot fight the bad guys
for twenty years.

You must know when to use force and when not to. If force must
be used, you have to win. You cannot come up second best; that
might come to mean dead. Death is real out there. People do not
get up when the director yells cut. You are not in a movie. There

is no music or six-minute commercial breaks to catch your breath. There is grunting, shouted orders, punching, stinky and sweaty grappling, and then hopefully the ratcheting noise of handcuffs.

When you do have to use force, you are allowed to go one level higher than an offender to subdue him. If he uses fists, you can use a nightstick, if necessary. If he pulls a knife, and if the threat to life is eminent, you can use a gun. The bottom line is that you do not have to fight fair.

Having said all that, my partner and I got a call of a disturbance. When we got the address, we knew what was going to go down. Whatever cocktail of drugs this guy took, he got very out of control belligerent, and his mother always called us. We knew it was going to be a fight from the get-go. "Crazy Momo" wanted to fight the police; we were his form of recreation.

We had a few guys like this in the district. He was one of the worst. He was a young and very fit guy—he could have posed in a muscle magazine. He could hurt you. The thing is, after we fought him, he would sleep it off in lockup. If he saw us when he was bonding out, he would apologize to us for acting out. Until the next time, and this was next time.

On this occasion, it happened to be my partner's turn. He would have to be the first man up a narrow, two-story stairway. Usually somewhere along this path, Crazy Momo would appear. Crazy was the operative word.

He stepped out of his door into the stairway. He had the advantage of being higher up than us. We tried talking to him, but he was already out of control, just fucking nuts. He was spouting Bible verses interspersed with curse words. He was doing Bruce Lee moves and making sounds like a strangled rooster. He was just fucking off-the-charts crazy.

As my partner approached, Crazy Momo lashed out with a karate kick to his chest. Thankfully, my partner was wearing his bulletproof vest. He grabbed Crazy Momo's leg. The fight was on.

There were fists, kicks, elbows, knees, and curses. It was a sweaty fur ball of nasty. We eventually overcame him, cuffed him, and not-so-gently dragged him down the stairs as he snarled at us.

We met Mom at the bottom of the stairs. She was tearful and probably wondering why she had wound up with such a crazy motherfucker for a son. But she loved him, and he straightened up a bit for Mom. We took him in for processing. He knew the drill. Mom knew the drill. Until next time. See ya, Crazy Momo. Slam. Clink. Crazy Momo died a few years later of a drug overdose. New crazies would rise to take his place.

MY TURN

We were working the wagon on afternoons, getting ready to head out for chow. Since we were allowed only a half hour for lunch, we figured we had better start heading to a restaurant before it got too crazy. If it was really busy, we couldn't take a lunch until it calmed down.

Sure enough, as we started to head out, we got a domestic disturbance call. We figured we would knock this job out then head for our bowl of beans. It was not to be.

It turned out that it was a newly divorced couple. The ex-husband had gone to his former home. Hubby discovered his ex-wife's "New Dude Jocker" was there. Hubby was deeply hurt, and New Dude Jocker was about to feel his pain.

Hubby opened up a can of New Dude Jocker whup ass on him. When that can was empty, he opened a can of pussy-ass humiliation on Mr. Jocker as he chased him down the street. We arrived shortly after Hubby had pulled his raging-bull act.

He was still on a testosterone high out on the front porch of a Chicago brick bungalow. He was talking to Wifey through the front window. She had called us because he would not leave. We tried talking to him, but he was still acting pretty aggressively.

We ascertained that she had gotten the house in the divorce, and we asked if she would sign a complaint against Hubby for criminal trespass. After she signed the complaint, we tried talking to Hubby, but fresh off his victorious thrashing of New Dude Jocker, he was not listening. My partner had already called for backup, and another wagon pulled up. All four of us tried to talk him down, to no avail. I was first on the stairway to the porch. I turned to my partner. He said, "It's you turn," and smiled.

I turned to Hubby. I told him we were through talking and he had to go. I took one step up the stairs. Hubby went into a crouch. He put his right hand behind his back as if reaching for a weapon. With his left hand, he gestured for me to come on up. He politely said, "Come on motherfucker. Come get some." I unsnapped my holster, as did the other officers. With my hand on my pistol, I took a step up the stairs. He retreated a step, still waving me up with the same refrain, "Come on motherfucker. Come get some." I advanced another step. He kept backing up. As I reached the porch, the hand behind his back came forward. It was empty. I rushed him.

He grabbed an aluminum-framed lawn chair from the porch and swung it at my head. I put up my arm to block it but was only partially successful. It gave me a glancing blow to the head, knocking off my glasses, which cracked as they hit the concrete porch. Now he was somewhat off balance. I pulled my nightstick and whacked him in the hand. He threw the chair. It bounced off of me.

He then started to throw punches. I again hit his hands and arms with the nightstick. His macho-man bullshit was starting to wear thin now. The other officers were also trying to subdue him. After a few more whacks with the nightstick, he gave it up. We piled on to cuff him.

We also had to make sure that he did not have a gun or knife in his belt. He had just tried to bluff four armed police officers with nothing. How stupid is that? That shit may have worked in a street altercation, but he overplayed that wolf ticket. He was lucky to be alive.

We never did find New Dude Jocker to sign a complaint for battery. We took Hubby in for criminal trespass, resisting arrest, and battery to a police officer. We advised an order of protection to Wifey. Now I had to get stitches in my left hand, an X-ray of my noggin', and new glasses. It had been my turn. No bowl of beans for me.

SQUEEZIN'

M ost police officers never fire their weapons in twenty-plus years of service to the city of Chicago. We do, however, have our weapons drawn on many occasions. Also on some occasions when a threat is eminent, we start squeezing the trigger.

At this point, when the hammer of a revolver starts to travel rearward, it does not take much more pressure on the trigger for the hammer to break forward. When the hammer falls, the firing pin at the front of the hammer strikes the primer at the rear of the cartridge loaded in the cylinder. The primer ignites the powder contained in the cartridge. In a controlled explosion, a bullet tightly contained at the tip of the cartridge is propelled down the barrel of the pistol in whatever direction that barrel is pointed.

When you are squeezing the trigger of a weapon pointed at an offender, his or her death or severe injury is just a nanosecond away. A somewhat similar process takes place with a semiauto pistol or a striker-fired pistol with some differences in pressure on the trigger and mechanics. The result is the same.

When you are squeezing the trigger, you are pretty sure that if you do not, either you or someone else is in mortal danger. This all happens in seconds. You must judge the threat and take action against it. Inaction may not be an option.

Citizens depend upon armed police officers to protect them. In many cases, you will be criticized if you act or don't act. In some cases, if you fail to act at a critical moment, your remains may get the big parade with the pipes and drums. Again, these decisions must be made in seconds. Shoot. Don't shoot. Here are some examples.

I was filling in for a guy on furlough who was a great police officer. His *set*, as he called it, was a foot patrol in a very busy area of commerce and criminal activity.

To paint a picture, here is a description of the area. There was a large liquor store with a parking lot usually filled with the "bottle in a paper sack" crowd. There was a halfway house for the mentally impaired, who during the day mixed with the population in the area. There was a single-room-occupancy hotel full of longtime residents. It also rented rooms to short-time occupants who needed more privacy than the street afforded (bust outs, drug users, drug dealers, prostitutes, gamblers, etc.). Two blocks away was another hotel. There was a shoeshine place with about ten chairs that was busy all day long. Nearby was a hardware store and a currency exchange. Several small fast-food places were interspersed in the mix. Four grammar schools and a high school added to the foot traffic. On top of all of this was a five-story YMCA with residents renting small rooms on a daily or weekly basis. There was also a busy elevated train stop with buses, cars, and commuter parking adding to the mix. In essence, the area made cat herding look organized.

I had to fill in for three weeks. I gave it a shot. In about a week, I developed kind of a snapshot of the area, the good, the bad, and the ugly. There was plenty of each. One fine summer day I was jib jabbering with a citizen near two elementary schools. The schools were on opposite sides of the street from one another. Most of kids were getting ready to rush the doors. I was hanging out on the corner to make sure they all got across the street safely.

There was a traffic light on the corner now. The officer I was filling in for got the city to put that light up after a kid was struck by a car and killed.

I was a half block away from a high school. The city had changed its name from high school to academy. I called it Statesville North; it was a prep school for the thug life. It had metal detectors at the doors. There were four police officers assigned to the school. At dismissal, four to six squad cars were assigned to make sure mayhem did not occur. The teachers there tried to do the impossible for the ungrateful but were only partially successful. Ten percent graduated. The rest went on to have their out-of-wedlock children and then get on the government dole. There were payments for every child out of wedlock. There were food stamps. There were WIC (women, infants, and children) payments. There was section eight subsidized housing. Who needed school? Who needed a job?

The young men quickly transitioned into slinging drugs for the major street gangs in the area. The teachers were saddled with pregnant teenage girls. They were hampered in their efforts to educate by a violent street gang culture. Some teachers, like some police officers, were just burned out. But, God bless them, they tried.

I heard car tires squeal around a corner near the high school. I turned. Coming toward me was a four-door junk. It was coming a little fast but slowed near the alley. An arm came out of the rear passenger's window. In the hand attached to the arm was a pistol. The pistol fired twice down the alley. Some kids on the sidewalk ducked as the car sped by. I grabbed my radio, called in shots fired, then gave my location. I pulled my pistol as the car approached the corner.

The civilian I was talking to disappeared. As the car came even with me, I stepped out from the corner. I leveled my pistol at the passenger in the rear seat and started squeezing the trigger. I shouted for the driver to stop the car. He did. Everybody in the car reached for the headliner. I eased up on the trigger. I told the driver to shut off the car. He did.

Momentarily, because of the heavy police presence at the school, several cars screamed up. The idiots in the car were not so gently ripped from it. Officers were tearing the inside of the car apart looking for the gun. The four chuckleheads were now laughing as they were bent over the hood of the car. The kid in the back seat was less than an eighth of an inch away from having his brains on the rear window. His eighth-grade graduation photo and his crying mama would have been on the five o'clock news.

But now this was funny. The officer searching the back seat found the gun. It was a starter pistol. I almost killed the fucking nitwit for a fucking starter pistol. I wanted to beat his ass into the ground then stomp on the bloody smear. I would have been justified in shooting the young thug. If they had not complied with my orders, I would have. A tactical team carted off the four. I finished my shift replaying this shit in my head on an endless loop. I had to eat my anger. That's healthy.

I was working afternoons and was as new as a shiny copper penny. I had not long before completed my probationary period. I was now able to work alone or partner with someone. The captain we had at the time did not like the idea of regular partners. He thought they would plot against him. What?

He was just a bit deranged. He would come to roll call inspections, which we had every day. His hair was uncombed, and his white shirt had gravy stains on it. His shoes were scuffed. Yet, he would criticize you for not having a sharp-enough crease in your pants.

Be that as it may, I was working with a female officer. She was newer and shinier than I. It was a busy night, and we were getting three jobs at a time. On top of this, everybody was trying to provide backup on in-progress calls. We were running a little crazy. I was trying to prove myself to the veterans on the job that I was carrying my share of the nightly circus. A man-with-a-gun call was broadcast. My partner and I were close, so we said we would take it. Most man-with-a-gun calls were crap. The callers were asked if the person they were calling about was armed. Many times, just to get us there quicker, they would say, "I think he has a gun." The callers knew that would guarantee a rapid police response. But usually the caller's problem was something like, "He owes me a quarter."

Usually when we arrived nobody would ever admit to saying that anybody had a gun when they did not have a gun. If they did admit it, we would arrest them for a false report, but those instances were rare.

When we arrived, we gave the other cars responding a slowdown as we were on scene. The location was a block of row houses. I met the caller, who was a woman in her mid-forties. I asked if anybody had a weapon. She told me no. It appeared to be a routine domestic disturbance, if there is such a thing as a routine domestic disturbance. At that point, I gave a disregard to other responding units.

No sooner had I given the disregard than the caller's husband appeared in the doorway with a gun in his hand. I drew my weapon and told him to drop the gun. He did not. I said "drop it" again and started to squeeze the trigger. Just then, his wife walked in front of my pistol. She told Hubby, "Put that gun down, you old fool."

I eased up on the trigger. Hubby ran inside the house. Fuck! I got on the radio again and said, "I have an offender with a gun; get me some cars over here." This was less than ten seconds after I had given a disregard. Real professional. Not.

My partner and I quickly took positions on opposite sides of the doorway. I yelled inside the door for Hubby to come out with his hands raised. No sooner had I said that than he walked out of the door like he was going to the store for a gallon of milk. He seemed surprised to see us, like the last few minutes never happened. I cuffed and searched him. No gun. I asked where he had hidden the gun. He said, "What gun?"

I guided him through the front door into the house. I kept asking. He kept denying. Other cars were arriving. Everyone was looking for the gun. I pulled Hubby aside and told him if he did not give up the gun, we would search every corner of his home to the extent that he would no longer be able to live in it.

As he watched officers methodically searching every cabinet and drawer in his kitchen, he got the picture. He said it was in the living room couch. I took him with me into the living room. It was as dark as the inside of an eight ball. I asked where the light switch was, and he told me the power had been cut off. Fucking great. Of course, my flashlight was in the car.

I gingerly felt around the couch cushions. I was worried about needles and vermin. Then I felt it. I told the other officers that the gun had been recovered. Hubby then told me that I could not keep the gun. He said his brother had brought it back from Germany after the war. It was a 9 mm German Luger. I said that I did not think the judge would give it back to him. He guaranteed me that the judge would.

"This guy must have had a degree in smartassery," I thought to myself. I was tempted to give the gun to his wife to let her kneecap him. We took him in, and as we were doing the paperwork, "Captain Gravy Stain" stuck his head in the interrogation room. He said, "Ah! A Luger. Nice pinch." He then picked up the Luger, disassembled it, and left.

By the time we were through with the paperwork, Captain Gravy Stain had left the building. Nobody in the station knew how to put the Luger together again. It was like a humpty-dumpty gun. Hubby told me he could put it together. By this time, I wanted to poke his fucking eyes out. We put the pieces of the gun into an evidence envelope. Our shift was thankfully over, a perfect end to a perfect day. PS He did not get the gun back.

I was working days when I was assigned to a call of a domestic disturbance with the brothers. When I was a kid, I fought with my brother continuously. Sometimes they were bloody fights. Yet no one ever called the police. In the 'hood, we got called for every kind of nonsense you can think of. The Chicago Police Department has a policy that it will send the police to every call no matter how ridiculous it may seem.

In the past, I had responded to an assignment in which the caller said that her husband would not go to work. Another caller said her son would not go to school. Ad infinitum. You might be asking, "What can the police do about shit like that?" The correct answer is that we cannot do a goddamned thing. Yet our time on patrol looking for real crime was limited by responding to these stupid calls.

When I was new in the department, I would wonder why some officers were so cynical. Now, I was them. The phrase "it's all bullshit" now made sense. We were babysitters to the ignorant. Get out of bed, drink your milk, listen to your mother—these are things I have said to imbeciles who can style their hair in forty different ways. They can wear a baseball cap in twenty different ways. Yet they cannot solve simple, everyday problems without police assistance.

They can also recite a complete rap song by Lil Wayne, but they cannot read or write. Granite has more of an IQ. That said, I was assigned a backup and started heading for the address of the domestic disturbance. Maybe this time it would be different. Maybe they would be arguing about quantum physics or the Fibonacci sequence. It was not to be.

Upon arrival at the multiunit apartment building, we trudged up the stairs to the third floor, like we had done a thousand times before. We heard loud voices at the door. We knocked, but the loud talking went on. One of the loud talkers came to the door while still yelling and let us in. We asked what the problem was. Are you ready for this? His brother was mad at him because he had eaten the brother's Maxwell Street polish sausage sandwich. What the fuck?

We migrated to the kitchen where there was no shortage of weapons. Bro number two was foaming at the mouth about Bro number one's food transgression. Bro number two had rolled out of bed at 11:00 a.m. salivating for said sandwich. When he found out Bro number one had eaten the sandwich, he flipped out. While we tried to calm the situation down, Bro number one taunted his brother.

He knew since the police were there, he would not be harmed. This was a common effect. Our presence sometimes would cause an aggrieved party or the protagonist to verbally abuse the other party, causing yet more conflict.

Bro number one must has said some really wrong shit that touched Bro number two's hot button. Bro number two grabbed a ten-inch knife from the sink. He advanced on his brother. I unholstered my piece and shouted, "Drop the knife or I will kill you."

He wisely paused in his advance. He looked down the barrel of my gun and dropped the knife. Now he had to go. We asked Bro number one to sign complaints, and he did. We knew this shit was going nowhere because they were family, but we had to get stupid away from stupider. A cooling-off period was in order.

If we did not make an arrest, we knew we would be back. Might as well get it over with while both parties were still alive. On the way out, we sympathized with Bro number two. No one should eat another man's sandwich. In some cases, it did lead to murder. We called them the pork chop murders. Only in the 'hood could a man be killed over a sandwich. We wondered with him whether a judge would have let him skate on a murder. Sandwich rights should be inviolable, we said. Bro number two agreed. We guaranteed him a nice sandwich of boloney and cheese. It did not have grilled onions like the Maxwell Street polish, but it would have to do. He said, "Thanks."

⟶⊹ ⊹⟵

I was working a one-man car on days. About eleven, I got a call to meet the revenue officer. I did not know what a revenue officer was, but I was going to meet him. I headed to the assigned address. I was about to collide with an "on-view" clusterfuck.

As I turned a corner near my assigned address, I saw a young couple on the sidewalk. At first glance they looked normal, but something was out of place. She was being hugged from behind by a street gang member. This was not in and of itself a criminal act, but in each of his hands was a woman's shoe. The teenage girl's feet were bare. It was a cool fall day.

I stopped the car and said, "Are you OK, Miss?" She did not answer; she seemed afraid. I spoke to him. I told him to let her go and to give her back her shoes. He told me that he had bought them for her, and he was taking them back. I let the radio zone operator know I had an on-view domestic. I gave the address. I told them I would handle my original call after I handled this.

I was now through being polite to this dickhead. I got out of the car and told him to let her go. He did. I told her to go stand by the car. She did. I said, "Now give her back her fucking shoes." He threw them to the ground. I gave them to the girl. I now told him to leave the area so she could walk home without being accosted.

He got on his child-size bicycle and rode to the corner less than a half block away. The gangbangers use children's bikes to pick up and deliver drugs and money.

I asked the girl what their relationship was. She said something I had heard hundreds of times before: "He's my baby's daddy." I asked how old she was. "Baby's Mama" told me she was fifteen. I asked why she was not in school. She said her baby was sick. I said, "Then why are you not at home taking care of your baby?" I got a blank stare.

This shit was not going well. I asked if she wanted a ride home. She declined. I turned to see "Baby Daddy" sitting on his bike on the corner, waiting for me to leave. I again told him to leave the area. He just gave me a hard stare. Then he stood up, letting the bicycle drop to the ground. Still glaring, he shoved his right hand down into his jacket pocket. This all happened in less than a second. I saw something black come out of the pocket. He brought it up waist high. I drew my pistol and shouted, "Don't do it!" I was squeezing the trigger with him in my sights. He then put a black cell phone up to his ear. I had almost killed him.

I took a breath and holstered my pistol. I started walking toward him. He picked up the bike, and I walked faster. He was a lanky nineteen-year-old, but he was trying to get going on a twelve-inch bike. I caught up with him in the middle of the street as he rounded the corner. I yanked him off the bike. He was going for disorderly conduct. He put up a struggle.

We wound up in some guy's front yard. I managed to get both of Baby Daddy's hands behind his back to cuff him. I had him by the jacket sleeves, but just then, two hands grabbed my right wrist. I lost my grip on his right hand. He jerked his left hand, snapping the tendon in my left little finger. At the time, I thought he had broken the bone because it went numb. I could not move it. The two hands that grabbed my right wrist were Baby Mama's hands. Wonderful. I managed to hang onto him.

The citizen whose yard we were in came out, and I told him to call 911 and say that a police officer needed assistance. He just stood there and did nothing. Eventually, I managed to get to my radio and called for an assist. Seconds later, the cavalry showed up. I locked up Baby's Daddy, Baby's Mama, and "Mr. I Ain't Going to Help No Police."

After the ER patched me up, I went into the station. I asked Baby Daddy whom he was calling on his cell phone. He said he was calling his lawyer. A nineteen-year-old with an attorney on call—go figure. The tactical guys who took him in told me he was a family member of the thugs who ran drugs on that street. Nasty people. That is why Mr. I Ain't Going to Help No Police stood there like a concrete garden gnome. He was probably scared to death of this kid. But you know, sometimes you have to check your nut sack. You have to stand the fuck up.

Baby Mama got referred to the juvenile officer, who sent her home. Mr. I Ain't Going to Help No Police got a slap on the wrist. Baby's Daddy got thirty days because of his habit of failing to appear for court dates. He had several warrants.

I later learned that the revenue person I was supposed to meet was a parking-enforcement car. They saw most of the incident, but they did nothing and left the area. When questioned why they did nothing to help, they claimed they saw nothing. They were not police, but they could have called 911 when they saw me struggling with Fuck Face. They didn't. When I thought later about the whole incident, I found that I had violated an old police axiom. I gave a fuck when it was not my turn to give a fuck. Lesson learned.

⇥⇤

I was working a one-man unit on days. A citywide call came out of man with a knife. I took a ride and was the first car on the scene. A young, muscular teen had a knife in each hand. They were not little knives; they seemed to me more like short swords. He was about thirty feet from me.

I drew my weapon and yelled at him to drop the knives. I saw no glimmer of understanding on his face. I started to walk toward him. He raised the knives, and I stopped. I yelled again to drop the knives. He did not. I was getting a little too close to the point where if he rushed me, I might get stuck. I did not want to get stuck.

It was daytime during the summer, and people were all over the street. Kids were playing everywhere you looked. This was not good. I raised my pistol. Again, I told him to drop the knives. He did not. I was going to have to do something. If this guy went bonkers, he could kill me or someone else. I yelled again for him to drop the knives. He did not. I started to squeeze the trigger when a voice near me said, "He deef." I turned to see an elderly man sitting on the stairs to my left. I said, "What?" like I was deaf. He said again: "He deef."

I took a chance. I holstered my pistol. He lowered the knives. Just then, other cars were pulling up. They saw an officer. They saw a guy with two knives. Everybody pulled their weapons. I shouted, "Don't shoot him; he's deaf." I motioned for him to drop the knives, and he finally did. We called for a wagon to take him to the hospital to be evaluated for mental problems. The trouble was none of us nor the ER staff knew sign language. If it were not for the citizen telling me he was deaf, he would have been headed for the morgue instead of the hospital. That would have been a more permanent loss of hearing. They say God looks out for fools, drunks, and the United States of America. I'm sure he fell into at least one of those categories.

━⊹⊹━

A call came out of "man with a knife." I was working a one-man car on days. I along with several other units responded to a multi-unit apartment building. It was one of those buildings that nobody wanted to go into. The apartments were small. Many times, they were occupied by ex-cons, felons, or crazies. There was no exception this time.

Someone in the third-floor hallway told us that this guy wanted us to shoot him—suicide by cop. We entered the tiny apartment and fanned out. There was about six of us plus "Mr. Kill Me," who was at the far side of the apartment near the windows behind a bed. He was about six feet tall with a lanky build and probably in his mid-thirties.

At first, he was threatening to kill himself with a large knife he held in his hand. We tried to talk him out of killing himself. His problem seemed to be over a woman, but his speech was rambling and incoherent. After a while, it seemed that he was getting angry with us and our efforts to stop him from killing himself. He was getting worked up to the point that we all thought he was going to charge us.

We all had our pistols out at our sides. I noticed as he became more irrational that several pistols were coming up and pointing at him. We were of one mind. We were going home tonight in one piece without any knife wounds. We would end his life before that happened, and if that is what he wanted, all he had to do was raise that knife and walk toward us. When it looked like he was going to do just that, everyone brought their pistols up in a two-handed combat stance. He took a step, and everyone started to squeeze their triggers.

Just then, a sergeant who had filed in behind us hit Mr. Kill Me full in the face with a stream of pepper spray. It was the best shot I had ever seen. I had no idea that pepper spray would shoot that far. Mr. Kill Me's hands went to his eyes. He dropped the knife. We piled on and cuffed him. Because he was acting so crazy and irrational, he won a free psych exam. He would be evaluated and medicated. That new young sergeant had saved his life, and we all went home in one piece. That was job one.

SQUOZE I

I was working a one-man car on days. It was almost 3:00 p.m., and I was about to head in for checkoff. A buddy and I were vegging out in a city park. It was a beautiful fall day in October 1992. Bill Clinton, one of the presidential candidates, was in Chicago looking for votes and money. My buddy and I were swapping stories and insults when we heard one of our friends get a job. It was a woman-with-a-gun call. We both thought it was bullshit, but we volunteered to back up our buddy. We thought the job would be coded out. The location of the call was near the station. After the backup, we would go in, check off, and then go home. It was not to be. We were scooting up to where our buddy was when he put out a description of an armed offender. We both hit the lights and sirens and stepped on it, cursing the drivers who got in our way. When we arrived, we got a quick update on the offender. She was a woman in her thirties wearing a long coat and armed with a revolver.

The backstory, we found later, was that the woman was a crack addict. She had several children, including an infant. Because of her drug habit, her own mother, the grandmother of the infant, had called DCFS to have her grandchild removed from the mother's care. To "Gunwoman," this was a loss of income. Without a job because of her addiction, each child earned her a government check. She had been living with an uncle because her mother had kicked her out of her home. The grandmother was raising Gunwoman's teenage daughter—this was not uncommon in the 'hood. The very thread that held the fabric of family together in the 'hood was the grandmother. Because of the hopelessness of her drug dependency and no foreseeable future, Gunwoman's plan was to kill her mother, her daughter, and herself. She took a loaded .38-caliber revolver from her uncle's dresser drawer.

She accosted her fifteen-year-old daughter on the way home from school and led her at gunpoint down the block to Grandma's house. She walked up on the front stairs with her daughter in the lead. Grandmother saw what was up and opened the door, grabbed her granddaughter, then slammed the door. Grandmother then called the police.

Here we were. At the time, we officers knew none of the whys and wherefores. We just knew we had a woman with a gun on the loose. We started at the last place she was seen. There was a small store just off the alley near Grandma's house. People at the store said they had seen her with a gun in her hand and that she had run into the alley.

We put out an updated description and gave our location. We knew other cars would be heading our way to tighten the circle. Because there was an elementary school nearby and school had just let out, there were kids all over the place. We had to find Gunwoman fast.

We split up. Each of us took a yard. I took a yard to the left. My buddies each took a yard to the right. There were many places to hide, plus the woman could dump her coat and blend into a neighborhood that she knew better than we did.

I had not gone very far when I heard one loud report followed by six more. I ran to the sound. I saw one of my buddies in the middle of a backyard. He was dumping his empty cartridges from his revolver and reloading. "Did you get her?" I asked.

He said, "I don't know." I asked where she was. He told me she was under the back porch just off a stairway leading to a basement door. I ran to the stairway, and just then, my other buddy was coming over an eight-foot fence in the yard next door. I still don't know how he did it; it must have been the adrenaline. I went down two stairs and saw Gunwoman. I fired two shots. I don't even remember the noise from the shots. Meanwhile, my buddy who had scaled the fence went up the stairs to the back porch, leaned over the railing, and fired two shots.

Just then, Gunwoman flipped out the gun. It flew in an arc like slow motion and clattered to the concrete at the bottom of the stairs. I still kept my revolver pointed at her. I did not know if she had another weapon. I passed her gun to my buddy, who was now right behind me. The gun barrel was still hot.

Gunwoman was lying very still. I thought we might have killed her. I poked here. She said, "Stop poking me motherfucker."

My buddy was on the radio calling for an ambulance. He called in "shots fired by the police." "No officers are injured. Start a supervisor heading this way," he said. All the police in the area converged. One of our buddies came running up. He had been blocking off the other end of the alley. He had run a full block at top speed to back us up. But it was over now. After Gunwoman called me a motherfucker, I dragged her out from her spot under the porch. She was cuffed. A CFD ambulance seemed to be there in seconds. As we helped to put her on to the stretcher, a crack pipe dropped out of her coat pocket. It would be inventoried. We searched her outer clothing. We found no further weapons or contraband. A car was assigned to escort her to the hospital. There a female officer would search her.

She would be guarded until she was sent to the county lockup. As it turned out, we had fired ten shots between us. She had been hit twice. I found out much later that my friend who had discovered her had tripped going down the stairs. It had saved his life. She fired at him, missing his head by inches. My buddy who was blocking the alley volunteered to do the paper.

We relocated to the district station. Our guns were taken, inventoried, and transported downtown to the crime lab. That was to make sure we were not using unapproved ammunition. Also, if ballistics were necessary, they would fire our guns and take note of the ballistics.

We were required to make statements to our supervisors. Our Fraternal Order of Police (FOP) representative gave us advice on how to word our statements, as we were giving up our rights to self-incrimination and counsel by being ordered to make a statement. If we did not make a statement, we could lose our jobs. The criminals had more rights than we did.

We finished that process, then we were required to be questioned at what was called a *round table*. This was to determine if our shooting of Gunwoman was justified. We were relocated to the area detective headquarters. There we were questioned by a host of agencies. I will try to list them as I remember them: the area chief of detectives, the deputy superintendent of the Chicago Police Department, our district commander, a representative from the Office of Professional Standards, a Cook County state's attorney, internal affairs, and an FOP representative. I may have missed some, but they were there to determine if we were justified in using deadly force.

After that, we were finally told we could go home. It was almost seven hours after the incident. I had the next two days off, but my buddies had to go to work the next day. We were all issued department revolvers until our revolvers were tested and returned. When the deputy superintendent went to interview Gunwoman in the hospital, she "motherfucked" him too.

Five months later, we were waiting to testify in court. We were in the jury room in the county building. It was a bench trial, and a judge would decide Gunwoman's fate. As it turned out, the women's restroom in the court was out of order. Gunwoman was led into our room to use the women's facility. On her way out, she asked, "Are you the officers I shot at?" We nodded. She said, "I'm sorry. I was high on drugs." We nodded.

She left the room with her Cook County sheriff escort. When her case was called, she pled guilty to attempted murder of a police officer. She received a mandatory seven years. I understand it is now fourteen years. Both of my buddies are now deceased; they were taken by cancer at a relatively young age. My buddy who did the report has just retired. I miss my friends every day. May God rest their souls. At the end of that day, by the grace of God, we all went home alive.

SQUOZE II

My partner and I were working "tac" (tactical team, civilian clothes) on afternoons. The gas pumps were down in our district, so we had to go to another district to gas up our unmarked ride. We were on the way back to our district when we monitored a citywide call of a man with a gun, shots fired. We were close to that address, so we figured we would take a ride.

We proceeded up a residential street. We were met by the caller, who said she had seen two men firing shots in front of a building not far from her own. Just then, two men came out of the building, and one of them fired some shots in the air. They had evidently not observed our stealthy selves standing there. We hustled the caller into her building and then went after the bad guys. They turned and ran into the apartment building with us in hot pursuit.

We caught up with them in the first-floor hallway. After a brief struggle, we conducted a pat-down search and recovered a .25-caliber semiautomatic pistol. We called the zone to let them know we had two in custody and to start rolling a backup. Simultaneously, the door of the first-floor apartment flew open. There had been a party going on, and the two dirtbags we had on the wall were part of it.

My partner turned to the partygoers and told them to stay away from us while I hung on to the two arrestees. The man who came to the door also had a pistol in his hand. My partner pulled his gun. The crowd in the apartment was shouting obscenities and yelling at us to release the two dirtbags. My partner told the man to drop the gun and put his hands on his head. The man fled into the apartment with my partner in pursuit. The gunman then grabbed a female occupant of the apartment by her throat, using her as a shield. Two men from the party jumped my partner after he followed the armed man into the apartment and knocked him to the floor.

Not long after, I heard the two shots. I released my hold on the two arrestees, and they took off. The gunman who had been holding the woman hostage had been trying to get a clear shot to kill my partner as he struggled with the two men who had jumped him. A backup had arrived just as the shots rang out and the two of us entered the apartment.

My backup went to the left, drawing his weapon on four men in the living room. I went to the right into the dining room. My partner had managed to fire two shots from the floor when he broke free from the men he had been struggling with. The gunman had thrown his hostage shield to the side and had taken a combat stance. He had been aiming his gun only inches from my partner's head. When my partner got off the two shots, the same two men who had been fighting with my partner fled. As they fled, they tried to prevent me from entering the dining room by holding a door that was blocking me. My partner had hit the gunman once, possibly twice. I forced my way into the room. the gunman was still pointing his weapon at my partner. I had a clear shot. I fired my weapon until the gunman was longer a threat. My last shot hit him in the head. He slumped into a chair. Dead.

It almost took longer to write this down than the actual incident took in real time. The whole incident start to finish took probably less than a minute and a half. The two guys who attacked my partner were taken into custody. They were both charged with aggravated battery. Ironically, the party in the apartment had been a birthday party. It turned out to be a death-day party. The bottom line was we both went home to our loved ones with no holes in us.

HEART BLOOD

We got a call of a disturbance in an apartment building. When we got there, trudged up the stairs, listened at the door, and heard subdued conversation. We also heard groaning near the door, so we knocked.

A woman answered the door, and we entered the apartment. Just inside the door was a man sitting on the floor. He was bleeding from a knife wound to his chest, but the wound did not appear serious.

I based my opinion of his condition on years of seeing a variety of stabbing and gunshot victims. It was kind of a first-responder triage. There were four people, including the woman who had opened the door, sitting at a kitchen table playing poker. The three men at the table were older, maybe in their mid-fifties. The man on the floor was in his early twenties. The woman was near the same age. The man on the floor kept yelling, "Look, it's heart blood" while showing us his blood-covered hand. We called for an ambulance but were told CFD paramedics were backed up with other jobs.

We asked the woman what had happened. She said she had broken off her relationship with "Mr. Heart Blood." We asked how he came to have a stab wound in his chest. Mr. Heart Blood, it seems, could not rationally handle the end of the relationship. He grabbed a knife and put it to his chest. He said, "Go ahead, kill me. Stab me in the heart. Kill me." She told us she tried to ignore him while she played cards with her relatives, but he kept up his rant. "Kill me. Stab me in the heart. Kill me." Ad infinitum.

After enduring his entreaties for fifteen minutes, she grabbed the hand that had the knife and pushed. The knife sliced into Mr. Heart Blood's chest. He screamed like a little girl, we were told. We really could not blame the young lady as Mr. Heart Blood's rambling was making us wish him silent.

We grabbed up Mr. Heart Blood, bid the young lady adieu, put him in our car, and left for the hospital. We got Mr. Heart Blood care for his "self-inflicted wound." We made our report.

We were ready for the next batch of the nightly nonsense. The dispatcher said, "Get your pencil out. Take these three." We wouldn't be doing any aggressive, preventative patrol; they had a backlog of never ending bullshit. We were gun-totin' garbage men in blue. Next.

THE EIGHT-HOUR MIGRAINE

Finding a partner is very difficult. One guy smokes, but the other doesn't. One guy likes the window open, the other doesn't. One guy wants to eat, the other doesn't. You get the picture. It takes a while to find someone compatible to spend eight hours with. Otherwise, coming to work is like an eight-hour tour in a Siberian lead mine.

Eventually, most everybody finds someone they can work with for an eight-hour tour. But there are some people with whom spending a shift with is like rubbing metal filings in your eyes. Being waterboarded might be more fun.

There was a female police officer who had some good days and some bad days. In a street disturbance, she would pick the biggest guy in the crowd and would poke her finger in his chest while questioning his relationship with his mother. You would then have to bat cleanup. That got old real quick. Most of the female officers were OK, but some thought they had to talk as tough as men. Their mouths would write checks their asses couldn't cash.

I once witnessed a female police officer get in an argument with a citizen in the district station parking lot. It got heated. She then yelled to a couple coppers in the lot to "arrest that man." We all just looked at her. She was wearing the same uniform we were. She was wearing a star. She had powers of arrest. We were like, "What the fuck? If you want him arrested, arrest him yourself." She didn't.

That said, one night it was my turn to work with "Officer Stone Bitch." We were working midnights (11:00 p.m. to 7:00 a.m.). It turned out to be one of her bad days. There basically was no conversation, and working eight hours with someone who does not speak makes the shift seem longer. Minutes crawl by. Officer Stone Bitch also never smiled either.

It was about 3:00 a.m. We were cruising at patrol speed down a residential street with our lights off. Near a large empty lot, we spotted a car with the motor running. No heads were visible. That may indicate several things.

The thought that someone may be having sex might involuntarily pop into your head. It would be a logical assumption. It might also mean a passed-out drunk sleeping in his car with the motor running. That might mean a person who would never again see the light of day. Or it might mean some sort of illicit behavior that may be drug related—for example, the post-heroin injection "nods" It could also be a stolen vehicle with or without occupants. All these things flash through your mind in milliseconds because you have run up against these types of things before.

We had to check it out. We hit the rear window with our spotlight. We did not hit the blue lights because that would have attracted a crowd of street zombies in less than five minutes, even at three in the morning. When that happened, you would have to watch the crowd plus the person or persons you were interrogating.

A head popped up, then two, then three. We called in our location and ran the plate. We unassed our vehicle. Officer Stone

Bitch took a spot near the right rear fender. I started to walk to the driver's side and saw the driver make a furtive movement as I approached. I pulled my pistol.

I told the rear-seat passenger to exit the car. When he opened the door, a cloud of marijuana smoke rolled out. I backed up a little, not wanting to get a contact high. I patted down the rear-seat guy. He was totally baked. I told him to get on the trunk.

Officer Stone Bitch had her pistol out too. It was up to her to have my back. She did. Next, I got the driver and passenger out of the same front door following the same routine. They were also buzzed. They had a kind of slow-motion stagger as they walked. They must have been tokin' on some primo shit. They both joined their pal with their hands on the trunk in the "front-leaning rest position" with legs spread. The front-leaning rest position is the first movement of the eight-count push-up. Demon drill instructors in the military use this to torture their charges by leaving you in said position until the muscles in your shoulders turn to jelly. Our modified position was not so severe but was meant to keep our suspects off balance while they were searched.

I cleared the rear seat, pulling it out of its clips to look under it. Nothing. As soon as I hit the front seat, I pulled my flashlight and looked under it. There among the desiccated French fries intermingled with Kentucky Fried Chicken bones, I saw the barrel of a gun. Woodsy Owl would have been proud that the driver had given a hoot by not throwing his garbage in the street.

I pulled the gun from under the seat. As I stood up, I said to Officer Stone Bitch, "Cuff 'em up." I displayed the gun to her, holding it by the butt with two fingers so as not to mess up any prints. She said, "Fuck you." That was at least two more words than she had spoken all night. She thought I was pulling an old copper's trick on her. Some old-timers would search a car after a rookie had searched it. They would then unholster their own gun and pretend to find it in the car the rookie had just searched. It was a form of friendly new-guy hazing.

I pulled my own gun to show her I was not fucking with her. She pulled her cuffs with a snarl. The three caballeros were so fucked up they could not have run even if they wanted to. Right now, their brains were moving in a super-slow-mo molasses mode. After searching the car, I was beginning to feel kind of Hostess-cupcake snackish myself. The whole stop took less than fifteen minutes. Only three hours and forty-five minutes to go. Now, because of my contact high, time was moving even slower. FA-UCK.

CROSSING GUARD

From time to time, a crossing guard would not show up because of an illness or a pressing family issue. When all other options to cover a crossing were exhausted, the crossing guard supervisor, a civilian, would ask for a police officer to be assigned to the crossing.

At the time, I was working a foot patrol and made it a practice to cross the children at the school on my beat. Because it was not on a main street, it was not a recognized crossing. That meant no one was assigned to it.

I found it useful to know the kids and their parents. Most of the kids were great. Because I knew their parents, I had fewer issues with bad behavior. A big plus was that if something wrong was going to go down, I would know about it beforehand. As Officer Fife would say, I could nip it in the bud. That tactic was working great, but as someone once said, "No good deed goes unpunished."

A lieutenant once told me that the better you do your job, the less the powers that be will think you are needed. If there was low crime in your area, they would not think it was because you were doing a good job; they would think because there was low crime that you did not need to be there. In essence, you would be a victim of your own success. He was right. I also violated the unwritten rule of never volunteering that I had learned in the military.

At the time that I had volunteered, I was part of a two-man foot patrol. Whenever they needed a man to work a car I volunteered. My partner had more time on the job, so I said I would take the assignment so he did not have to. Now I was working a one-man foot patrol, but I was still thought of as the go-to guy since I had volunteered before.

The day before, I had given a talk to eighth graders on my beat telling them I would be by their school every day. I told them if they had a problem with any threats or violent behavior, I would be there to help. The next day, I was called in to see the watch commander. One of the crossing guards was pregnant. Because of red tape, they could not hire another crossing guard because they had a full complement. She would not be able to work for seven months. Guess who was going to take that corner for the next seven months? You got it pals and gals. It were me.

It was an hour and a half in the morning then an hour in the afternoon. Wonderful. I was to start the next day. A day after I told a classroom full of children I would be there for them every day, I would be somewhere else. I argued my case to the watch commander. I was told it was a manpower thing. My arguments fell on deaf ears. The next day, I was on the corner.

There was no traffic light at the corner. To cross children, you had to wait for a break in traffic. I would stop the southbound traffic, then wait for a break in northbound traffic and stop them. Then you could motion the little tykes across the street. The crossing was about midway between a high school and an elementary school. In the morning, I had the little ones going east, teens going west. In the afternoon, the reverse. Most of the teens avoided the corner. They did not want to be around the police. I got that. The little ones were fine with very few exceptions.

I initially had some friction with the drug dealers, their lookouts, and their security. I went to where I thought most of the activity was being run from. I told them I did not expect to see them slinging drugs while I was out there crossing kids. I could not permit young children, some with their parents, to see a Chicago Police officer standing a half block away while they sold drugs. We came to an understanding. They moved their operation out of my sight while I was on that corner. I told them that if they did not, I would bring the full weight of the department down on them. If that did not do it, I would call the Feds. If that did not work, I would call in the 82nd Airborne. They got the picture. They were running a business.

I only had trouble with one guy from another drug crew on my side of the street. Their corner was out of my sight, but their *security* kept circling the block with his cell phone. We had words. He was uncooperative. I could not leave the corner while kids were crossing—I could not take the chance that some little kid would be hit by a car. I called in some tac guys. He got the message. After I got that straightened out, my biggest problem was the weather.

Spring and fall were not bad, but summer and winter were sometimes pretty brutal. Because I was a foot patrol, I was used to the weather. But on foot patrol I could move or take shelter. On a crossing, you could not leave the corner. Time goes pretty slow when it is ball cold, snowing, or raining buckets. The corner was in a residential neighborhood. I had two empty lots behind me with nothing to block the wind. The other three corners had houses on them. There was no shelter from sun, wind, rain, or snow. I developed a new appreciation for those crossing guards. Also, I found they could be a great source of information if you had to use them. But because they were women and men alone on busy corners, you did not want to put them in jeopardy by turning them into snitches.

A few people in the neighborhood came by to thank me for what I was doing. They were especially appreciative of the curtailing of the drug trade so the kids did not have to deal with it. I thought since I was going to be there anyway, I might as well do something to make the time pass.

I noticed the corner I was on had a sidewalk that was literally in pieces. It was so bad that women pushing infants in strollers as they walked with their school-age children had to use the street instead. This put them in traffic. I called Streets and Sanitation to see if they could replace the sidewalk. I was told that I would have to call the alderman to put it on the schedule. I called the alderman, who was a woman. After some jerking around with her staff, I was able to speak to her. The first question she asked me was, "Why are you calling me?" I explained that I was told she had to put the sidewalk repair on the list for it to be done. I explained that women with small children had to walk in the street because the sidewalk was in such bad condition. She said she would take it under advisement. That was Chicagospeak for "do not call here again."

When I left the district years later, nothing had ever been done to repair that sidewalk. The "City That Works" only works if you have clout. Those women did not have clout. I did not have clout. That was that.

I think my worst moment on the corner was not the weather, the gangs, or the kids. We had just gotten a new district commander, and he was being driven around the district by one of the underbosses. The weather was brutal. A blizzard was raging in typical Chicago fashion. I was covered with snow and ice. They stopped their vehicle on my side of the street but on the opposite corner. I glanced over. They were laughing. After a while, they cruised up to me still laughing. They cracked the window about three inches and asked how it was going. I was standing on an unprotected corner in a fucking blizzard. I was covered with snow and ice. I would be there for another hour. I said. "Just fine" through the icy scarf covering my mouth. They left. I had a few uncharitable thoughts. I shook off the snow and soldiered on. So, if you see crossing guards standing out there in the rain or snow, give them a friendly wave or a thumbs-up. They deserve it.

UH-OH

My partner and I were working afternoons. It was a hot day, and we had no air. The car was like a fucking sauna. We were both new on the job. We were still learning the street. It was a long process—it took years. We were assigned to a man-with-a-gun call.

We pulled up next to the apartment building and unsnapped our weapons just in case this call wasn't bullshit. As we reached the first landing, a door opened. There was a frightened face in the opening. We asked if he had called. He said he did. We entered the apartment. This guy was really scared. He told us he had gotten into an argument with the three guys who lived across the hall. They had threatened to kill him. He kept saying, "They got a gun. They got a gun." We had to tell him to shut the fuck up.

We needed more information before we went storming over there: descriptions, type of weapon, where the exits to the apartment were, etc. But suddenly, we heard a loud report, and the wooden door through which we had entered splintered. We pulled our pistols, heard the door across the hallway slam shut. We called in shots fired. The cavalry was on the way.

We could not shoot through doors with no clearly defined threat. We exited the apartment and booted the door across the hall. The three nitwits inside looked surprised to see us. We roughly put them into the search position on the wall while yelling at them to give up the gun. They acted like we were crazy. That made us even angrier. After all, they could have killed one of us when they shot through the door across the hall.

When they denied shooting through their neighbor's door, we got even angrier.

The cavalry was on scene now. The apartment was being systematically searched. It wasn't pretty. Our sergeant showed up. We described to the sergeant exactly what had happened. He looked at the outside of the door where it had been shattered. He determined it had not been damaged by gunfire—the hole was too big and too round. The sergeant then looked in the nitwits' apartment and found a hammer near the door. The hammerhead fit perfectly into the hole. Uh-oh!

The cavalry started to leave as fast as they had come. Suddenly, we were as alone as a snake in Ireland. Just then, an officer came out of the bedroom with a snub-nose revolver. He found it hidden behind a radiator. I could have kissed him. That must have been the gun our victim was threatened with. I guess all's well that ends well. But without that gun, we would have been in a world of shit.

Thank you for your largesse in helping us find that gun, oh God of helping new coppers un-fuck themselves.

FIRES

Outside of war, there is probably nothing worse than a fire. It will take the breath from your lungs. It will boil your eyeballs. It will painfully bubble your skin and blast the hair from your body.

In our area, there were a lot of fires. Many of them were in the winter. It seemed like nobody was happy with the heat provided by landlords. In almost every apartment during a cold spell, it was so hot you could not breathe. To push back the cold, all four burners on a stove would be on. The oven would be on. Space heaters would be on. It was a firefighter's nightmare.

The CFD guys were always great. They went places that would scare a normal human being out of his wits. And they made it look easy. We would respond to the fires with them. We were there to block off traffic so they could carry out their tasks. Believe it or not, some dummies would actually drive over fire hoses while a fire was raging. We also dealt with the losses incurred by completing a report for the displaced owners. Also, at some scenes while firefighters were risking their lives to bring a fire under control, we had fire trucks looted for brass hose couplings or tools. As an added insult, firehouses were also looted on occasion to the point where people had to be left behind as security. It's hard to believe but true. In another vein, we had a cadre of pyromaniacs who thought arson was a fun way to spend an evening.

At one scene of multiple garage arsons, I asked one of the firefighters the status of the fire. He referred me to another firefighter. It turned out the first guy I spoke to was actually the arsonist. He was dressed like a firefighter who stayed with the truck, usually the engineer who dealt with water pressure on the pumpers. The arsonist was walking around with a flashlight. He looked like a firefighter. Seven garages burned that night. He was probably at every scene.

Guys like that get a thrill in their special place from fire. It's even better if they can pretend they are firefighters. By the time I figured it out, the arsonist was in the wind. I put out a description, but no more fires occurred that night. He probably had police and fire scanners; he knew we were looking for him. Arson, by the way, is one of three common traits found in serial killers. The other two are cruelty to animals and bed-wetting. Was our arsonist predisposed to homicide? We would know only if we caught him. We never did.

In my career, I came on only a few fires "on view." Usually the fire trucks were on scene before we got there. I came upon one fire while I was on routine patrol. As I rounded a corner, flames were already blasting out the front door of the house like a blowtorch. I notified the zone to start rolling the trucks to my location. I went to the front stairs, but the heat was so intense I could go no further. The smoke eaters got there minutes later. They quickly got the fire under control. Unfortunately, the house was a total loss. That usually meant another abandoned house or empty lot on the horizon.

Another problem at fire scenes was with board-up contractors. The board-up contractors also had scanners, and they showed up at almost every fire. Many times, they got in the way of police and fire functions. They knew the houses usually had insurance, so the board up would be covered. There is no doubt these buildings needed to be boarded up. The scavengers would descend like vultures to strip whatever was of value, such as copper piping, copper wiring, aluminum gutters, etc. I used to keep the board-up contractors from the scene until all fire and police were gone from the area. They were not happy, but I was not there to make them happy.

Another fire I came upon while on patrol had not yet erupted to a blaze. I saw smoke rolling out the front door of the house. I called it in and ran up the front stairs. There was a wall of smoke blocking the entrance. I got on my knees. I could see into the house under the layer of smoke. There was no smoke from the floor up to about a foot high. I contemplated crawling in under the smoke but decided against it because of the heat coming from the structure. Plus, it scared the shit out of me.

As it turned out, there was no one in the house. The firefighters did find where the fire started, however. It was in a closet. It appeared that the eight-year-old who lived there had been playing with fireworks in the closet. When the fire started, he ran from the house. I found him outside, and he told me what had happened. His father showed up after the firefighters had left while I was filling out my report referencing his son's statement. He was one very unhappy man. He could not believe his son was the cause. I'm pretty sure some serious heat was going to be applied to his son's butt in the near future. The good thing was that no one was hurt.

Another fire that sticks out in my mind was in a multiunit building. I think one of the chiefs said it was a four-alarm fire. It was winter, nighttime, and nut-shrinking cold. When it is very cold, ice, steam, and smoke become problems. Everything in the vicinity of the fire-hose spray became covered with ice, including the firefighters. Besides dealing with the smoke, the steam created by cold water hitting hot surfaces compromises your vision. I was still pretty new on the job. I called for a Chicago Transit Authority (CTA) supervisor to send a bus for the families displaced by the fire; they were standing in the frigid weather in whatever they grabbed on the way out the door.

You could barely see the three-story building because of the smoke and steam. Several apartments had been totally involved. Many more had been damaged by water and smoke. It was a real nightmare. While I was out there, I started hearing a dinging sound like an alarm clock coming from inside the building. Then I heard another, then another. I asked one of the firefighters what the hell that sound was. He told me it was the sound of the firefighter's oxygen tanks running low. In a little while, the whole building sounded like a giant alarm clock.

The firefighters performed many rescues that night. As the fire advanced, people were hanging out windows. Some jumped. Needless to say, some were injured. There was an ambulance on scene, and the paramedics called for more help. A short while later, the fire was struck. There had been one fatality, a man on the third floor. He was in the apartment at the fire's origin. I was told it appeared that he had started to cook something, and he probably fell asleep. He may have died of smoke inhalation, so I was told by one of the chiefs. I called for a wagon to transport the fatality to the morgue. The medical examiner would determine the cause of death.

Meanwhile, a firefighter led me into the building to where the fatality was found. He called the deceased a "crispy critter." I suppose that was a little firefighter humor. All these guys had just risked their lives to get to this guy to save his life. But, like police officers who deal with violent death pretty often, they too have their way to cope with it. It was a dark humor, but it helped us deal with the daily carnage.

The firefighter led me up to the third floor and into an apartment. I could not see anything except his back and some reflective material on his uniform coat. A flashlight was very little help in the smoke and steam, which just reflected the light back into your eyes. He suddenly stopped and said, "There he is." I could not see anything. I could not even see the floor. I said, "Where?" My question was met with silence. The firefighter had left. I shouted out. Again, silence. I was alone with a burnt corpse that I could not see, in a room in which I could not define any shape. I was a blind man with no clue at all to my location in the apartment.

I shouted out again. Nothing. Now I was getting a little panicky. I did not want to join "Mr. Crispy" on the floor. I yelled out again. The firefighter came back, chuckling at my discomfort. I had been pranked. In payment for their mirthful behavior, the smoke eaters bagged the corpse. They carried him down three flights of stairs, saving us the task. It was a nice payback.

Thank you, God of the CFD, for having such fine individuals in your service. In my own personal experience, whenever I called them to bring me a ladder or bucket to search a roof for a gun or a burglar, they were there. If we needed help with a body, they were there in minutes, even at three in the morning. They truly are, among other things, Chicago's bravest.

SHOULDN'T YOU BE EATING DOUGHNUTS SOMEWHERE?

I was filling out some date and signature boxes in my parking ticket book before walking up the street. There were still parking meters on the beat. I thought the meters were a detriment to the businesses along the street. Why would you stop at a business where you had to feed a meter to shop? A counter to that narrative was that people in the area would be able to leave their cars there indefinitely in front of a business. But the city wanted in your pocket any way it could.

Being in your pocket meant more money available to buy votes and thus stay in power. Keep those coins rolling in—cigarette tax, gasoline tax, sales tax, liquor tax. If they could, they would tax you per breath. Well, parking meters were revenue, and I was a tax collector. I did not like writing tickets to people who mostly could not afford them. I could understand if the parking violations were hazardous, like blocking alleys and driveways or double parking. But until I was elected mayor, I had a job to do. Police officers do not always agree with the laws we enforce. Sometimes it seems some laws are just plain stupid. The laws are instituted in the legislative branch of government, and we are not the duly elected representatives of the people; we are the enforcers. So, enforce the laws we must.

I was a foot-patrol officer at the time. I was using a tire shop as kind of a community policing office. The owner was a supporter of the police. He appreciated the work we did in the community. There were several young, hard-working guys working there. Every once in a while, some of their friends would wander in to say hello. Some were fans of the police, some not.

One of the non-fans walked in that particular day. He saw me and said, "Hey, shouldn't you be eating doughnuts somewhere?" I gave him my best Tyrannosaurus Rex grin. He shut up. He now was in my "you had better not fuck up" rolodex. I later learned his name and that he had a proclivity for acquiring property that was not his own. Based on that info, I ran him for a sheet. He had done a little time in one of our state-supported gray-walled institutes. You wonder how stupid somebody could be to intentionally call attention to his felonious self. Maybe it was not even stupidity; maybe it was wiseassery.

Well, about a year went by. A Cook County sheriff stopped by the tire shop one day. He was looking for "Mr. Wiseass," who was a fugitive from justice. I told the sheriff that if I saw him, it would be my pleasure to take him into custody. Not two weeks later, I was working with a PPO. We were smokin' and jokin' down the street. From about a block away, I spotted Mr. Wiseass. He was with a woman who at that time I did not assess as a threat.

I alerted the recruit to follow my lead. As we neared Mr. Wiseass, I grabbed both of his arms from the front. I told the PPO to cuff him up. His girlfriend bolted. I later found out that she had warrants. I said, "I was just on my way for some doughnuts, and there you are, a fugitive from justice. You must have pissed off the police doughnut God." Just an FYI—there was not one doughnut shop in the whole district. There was not even a bakery. So, if you really wanted a freshly baked doughnut, you had to go out of the city to get one.

I turned Mr. Wiseass over to the sheriff. They wrote us up for an "attaboy." About two years later, I ran into Mr. Wiseass again. He was a changed man, so he said. He had time to reflect on his previous criminal past. He was going to be on the straight and narrow from now on. I wished him luck. Every parolee I have ever spoken with upon their release says basically the same thing when they get out of the joint. It is like a script they memorize.

About five months later on a shitty wintery day, I spotted Mr. Wiseass, his girlfriend, "Ms. Sprinter," and a new cohort in crime. They were double parked in front of the secondhand store (criminal fencing operation). The trunk of the car was open. A TV, CD player, CDs, and other electronics were visible. As I approached, Ms. Sprinter took off at a high rate of speed. I put Mr. Wiseass and "Mr. Friend" in the front-leaning rest search position. I cuffed them together since Mr. Friend looked like he would die while sprinting.

I called for an assist. I asked the zone if there were any recent reports of burglaries. That was negative. I asked them to check the surrounding suburbs. A few minutes later, they told me an officer in a suburb adjacent to my beat was taking the report as I spoke. I listed the items that were visible in the trunk. A few minutes later, the zone came back with an affirmative response. Bingo. The suburban officers came and carted away Mr. Wiseass and Mr. Friend for burglary.

I ran into Mr. Wiseass's brother some years later. I asked about Mr. Wiseass. His brother told me he had died of AIDS in prison. The unsavory-brown-doughnut-hole God had taken him. I never saw Ms. Sprinter again, at least I do not think so. She had a decent-sized rapper but no picture. In both encounters with her, all I remember was a fleeting profile and a cloud of dust. She had, for the time being, escaped the wrath of the doughnut gods.

ANOTHER CAPER

One fine December day, I was on aggressive/preventive patrol. One of the kids near the steps of the local elementary school flagged me down. I had spoken to him before. He had been threatened by one of the other kids who waited for the school bus at that location. On this occasion, he told me the same kid had threatened him with a gun.

I knew the kid in question. He was a hard case. Although young, he had that hard-ass gang member look. "Mr. Hard Case" had engaged me in a stare down when I told him not to bother anyone at the school. He was fourteen then but was already on the way to a life of runnin' and gunnin', incarceration or death. I knew where he lived. I called for an assist.

One of my old partners was working the burglary car. He was on the way to my patch to investigate a burglary. I told him I would meet him and his partner at that address. The burglary had occurred next to the young Mr. Hard Case's house. Yikes. We all deduced that my guy could have done it.

I went to Mr. Hard Case's garbage receptacle. There under some trash was a jimmied strongbox. We knocked on the door where the burglary occurred. A young lady I knew who had attended the elementary school on my beat answered the door. I asked her if the damaged strongbox was hers. She said it was and asked where I got it. When I told her, she was shocked.

Mr. Hard Case had grown up next door to her. They were friends. He knew her mother, father, and the family dog. They had him over for lunches and dinners; he was like one of the family. You could tell she was hurt. I asked where he got in. She took us to a basement window that he had slithered through. The window was between the two houses. He had probably unlocked it on one of his visits. Because he knew their dog, it made it all the easier.

It had been a major burglary, including the wedding ring of a grandmother who had passed away. There were rare coins and jewelry, including rings, gold chains, and watches. It was all worth more than $5,000—a pretty big score for a sixteen-year-old.

We went back to Mr. Hard Case's house. His parents gave us permission to search his room. We found a .32 caliber pistol in a toy box. His parents were good people; they could not believe their son had a gun. They also could not believe he burglarized the neighbor's home.

I knew what gang Mr. Hard Case was in. I called in a few favors and got an address in a suburb where he was hanging with other gang members. He was at the home of one of the gang's high-ranking members. I had chatted with this gang member before, and he was also a hard case. He had been shot in the shoulder on one of our corners. He refused all cooperation with police and medical treatment. He just held a T-shirt over the wound and walked home.

We called the suburban police department to let them know we were coming into their jurisdiction. One of their cars met us. All the coppers I ever worked with from that town were good people. We went to the gang leader's home. Fortunately, his uncle answered the door. He was a regular guy, and he let us in. We asked where our guys were. He led us to the basement stairway, and we walked down the stairs. Surprise! They were toking on some weed.

We harshed their mellow. Not bueno. There were five of them, including our guy. Mr. Hard Case confessed to the burglary, and we took him in. He felt contrition. I let him use the telephone. Within the hour, we had all but one ring brought to the station. We even had some bonus stuff. He and another gang member had gone on a buying spree. They had used the victim's two credit cards to buy some gold chains and gold rings.

My buddies cleared the burglary, we took a gangbanger's gun off the street, and we got back most of the loot. All in all, it was a pretty good day for the men in blue.

HUH? WHO, ME? I

We were rambling down the street in the one-ton boneshaker—the wagon. I was working with a PPO who was a really good guy. He was smart and tough. Usually, if you had the first attribute, you did not have to use the second as much. In our job, though, you had to reason with the unreasonable. You had to try to talk logic to the illogical. So your physicality was always a desirable attribute to bring to the table if logic and reason proved irrelevant.

I was his FTO. By the time the PPOs came to us to complete their training, they were usually a little apprehensive about this next step. They wanted to get out there to do what they were trained to do. Usually, it did not take them much time to conclude that they really did not know anything about being a police officer. They just had the basics. We all went through the same period of acclimation. It took a while to get "the street," sometimes years.

This was only a beginning. I, as a rule, told them to forget all that FTO and PPO crap. We were now partners. School was over. Scenarios were over. In five minutes out on their first day, we could be killed by a bad guy who did not give a fuck about them being the new guy. You would not get a do-over.

We FTOs were just guides. I had also grown as a teacher of sorts. Years before, my father had made me teach him algebra. He had little need for algebra, but he cleverly made me learn it well enough to teach him. So being an FTO made me a better police officer. Kudos to the instructors in the department training academy for giving me such good people to train further. I never had a bad one.

That said, we were working afternoons. It was a busy day. My PPO spotted a punched trunk lock on an Oldsmobile Cutlass. All right! At the time, it was a target model of car that everybody was stealing whether for parts or joy riding. We hit the lights and gave the siren a short squeal. The driver panicked and hit the gas. Off we went. He drove about a half block, curbed the car, and bolted on foot.

My PPO was already savvy enough to stay with the car to disable it. One of the things you learn as a new guy is that if you both take off after the runner, either the runner doubles back or some neighborhood opportunist will re-steal the car. Even though he had a jump on me, I started to close in on the runner. Then I saw him bolt up some stairs and into a house. I really was not expecting that.

I followed him up the stairs into the house. I pulled my revolver. I did not know if the runner was armed, and I did not want this day to be my last. As I came through the front door, I heard other units responding. I was in a darkened living room of a Chicago bungalow. In the kitchen, I saw a woman reading a paperback book while sitting at the kitchen table. I said, "Excuse me, did a man run through your house?"

She asked, "What did he do?"

I related he had bailed out of what we thought was a stolen car. She barely looked up from her book and said, "He in there."

It was a small, dark bedroom off the kitchen. At first, I did not see anything but a bunk bed. As my eyes became accustomed to the dark, I saw a large lump in the bottom bunk. I poked the lump. The lump moved. I told the lump to get out of bed. He asked, "Huh? Who me?" He was squinting like he had just woken up. I peeled back the covers, then said, "Do you always sleep wearing your jacket and shoes?" Again, the ubiquitous "Huh?" I cuffed him.

I told Mom that he would be at the district station. He was only sixteen. She had to come in to the station because he was a juvenile. She said, "Let the fool sit." She did not even look up from her book. Mr. Lump was crestfallen. He knew Moms was mad. The juvenile justice system would probably send him home with Mom. His punishment would probably be against the law.

My partner was back at the car arranging for a tow. The car was a steal. We put Mr. Lump in the wagon. He was crying big tears. A car was assigned to the steal to make sure it was still there when the tow truck came. We took Mr. Lump in for processing. When we were done, we put him into the detention cell where he would wait for the youth officer and Mom.

When we left after our shift, he was still in there. I do not think he wanted to go home with Mom. I think he would have preferred to go to juvenile detention. I think Mom was going to put some lumps on Mr. Lump.

HOBOS!

We were looking for a killer. He was a pimp and had killed one of his girls. We were not sure why. It could have been many pimp reasons. Perhaps she no longer wished to fellate tricks for money. Perhaps some of his personal dope was missing. Perhaps she held back a little money. All good reasons for murder in piece-of-shit pimpland.

We had heard our suspect was hiding out in some sort of hobo jungle. Go figure. We went down where the majority of whores worked. It was on a major street with two traffic lanes and a parking lane near a major expressway. The expressway facilitated the quick on and off of the tricks, without the necessity of driving through the rest of the 'hood. Driving through the 'hood late at night looking for whores could get you killed. That is no bullshit. If you doubt that, get in your Lexus or Mercedes convertible, drive down there, and ask for a whore. Flash a wad of cash. Wear some nice bling. Whether you contributed to the United Negro College Fund will never come up. You will be deprived of your property, and you may be deprived of your life if your depriver thinks you can identify him in a lineup. If you doubt, go see.

That said, we were just some blue shirts acting on a tip. We were on the main drag under a railway bridge. We climbed up the concrete walls that supported the bridge. That was fun, as we all wanted to scuff our boots and dirty our uniforms. But the job was the job, so we did it while grumbling our distaste for murderous pimps. After we surmounted the wall, we walked a path through some vine-like trees. Then we started to see something we had never seen before: there were discarded bloody hypodermic needles everywhere. We were freaking out as none of us wanted to get stuck.

Needless to say, AIDS and hepatitis C were foremost in our minds. The needles were on the ground and stuck into the tree trunks. It was like "Hypodermicapaloozaville." After we got through the trees, we came upon a little village of railroad-tie shacks. As we ungraciously rambled around, some whore faces peeked out at us. They were using sleeping bags and mattresses to lay their weary heads. There were no men in Hypodermicapaloozaville. They were probably nodding off in some fleabag motel along that strip or dividing up heroin for their whore slaves. But that's a story for another time.

We gathered the female residents of Hypodermicapaloozaville. We told them our reason for visiting their fair whore village. They knew the guy we were looking for. They knew the girl whom he had killed. They said he had not been around; they heard he was in Michigan. We looked in every hobo shack because although we knew that heroin-addicted prostitutes would not lie to us, we thought the murdering pimp might have slipped in without their knowing. Hmm. Satisfied that he was not there, I left a card with a number to call in case he came back.

As we were leaving, I asked, "Why are you girls living with a bunch of hobos?" One girl stepped up. After looking over both shoulders, she whispered "Hobos! They are not hobos. They are bums. They get mad if you call them hobos." We were kind of stunned that our choice of language made so much difference. Not wanting to compromise our investigation by some smartass remark, we said nothing. We carefully left the village of Hypodermicapaloozaville.

Upon my return to the station, I called the railroad police. Yes, there is such a thing as the railroad police. They said they would reclaim the village. They used the railroad to deliver a bulldozer to Hypodermicapaloozaville. The village, like ancient Carthage, would be relegated to the ash heap of history. Eventually the pimp we sought was caught, convicted, and sent to prison. Thank you, God of Dead Whores. Case closed.

VIOLATIONS

K ids in the 'hood grow up like any other kids in America until they are about seven. They run, they play, they wonder about girls. Then their lives, in many cases, take a nasty turn. The major street gangs in the area start recruiting. They need the "young uns" to add members to the gang.

A gang lives on recruitment. Its members are tasked with recruiting new members through example or intimidation. Recruits are needed because many of the gang's middle management and corner crews go to jail or prison or are killed. New blood is needed to keep the multibillion-dollar drug trade machine humming along. They target the young because to the young, "thug life" seems glamorous and exciting.

Many of these kids in the 'hood have either no father or the father is in jail or unknown. The gangs mentor these kids. They tell them that book learning is for chumps. The real money, thus power and respect, is in the drug trade. The kids buy into it due either to threats or willing acquiescence.

First the kids start out by doing small tasks. They act as look-outs to alert the corner crews of police or rival gang crew activity. They may act as runners transporting drugs, money, or weapons to corners. The gang leaders count on the police not stopping children on bicycles. They are given money or stolen items for their performance.

When they hit high school age, they are then full-fledged gang members. They are disruptive, violent influences that dumb down the learning process for others. Many teachers are fearful of disciplinary procedures against the gang members. The teachers are in classrooms filled with gang members or gang sympathizers. The gang members are socially promoted until they are old enough to quit school at sixteen. Then they go to work.

If you went for a job and then were told you would be doing ten to twelve hours on a corner in all seasons, even if it meant working in one hundred degrees to twenty below zero, would you take that job? If time off was not decided by you but by the need to staff the corner, would you take that job? If you were told you must show up for work regardless of a valid excuse, would you take that job? If you were told you might be murdered or sent to prison because of your occupation, would you take that job? If you were told you might also be subject to discipline from your employer should you come up short on money or drugs, would you take that job? Most rational people would not take a job for which such probabilities existed. But we are not talking about rational, logical, thought-ful human beings. If you are one of the dunces who would risk employment in a drug crew, and you messed up, that would be considered a violation.

The discipline dispensed would depend on the severity of the infraction. Not doing what you are told or talking out of turn may get you a violation called a *punkin' head*. The punkin' head occurs when you are beaten so badly that your head swells. Even your mama may not recognize you. If you survive that, the boss may let you work again. Would that ever happen at Mickey D's? Not likely without a police report, an arrest, and a lawsuit. Try suing the dope man and then see what happens to you and your family.

Another violation up the ladder is "the cripple," as in "cripple that motherfucker." This discipline is pretty severe as it will results in one or more of your bones being broken. You may be shot in an elbow or knee. You will live as an example to those who may think they can cut the package to keep some money for themselves or skim some money from the count. They may let you live as a message to others. They may not. Do you think Burger King would shoot you or hit you with a baseball bat for skimming some little money from the cash drawer? I think not.

Farther up the ladder is "trunked," a major violation. Perhaps you want to usurp a more powerful gang member or the gang leader. You may simply disappear, just a picture on a milk carton. If a message is to be sent, you may find yourself with a duct-taped mouth, hands, and feet. You may find yourself in the trunk of a stolen car. You may find the trunk rather warm as they have set the car on fire. Adios, usurper.

Such is the result of a thug life. Sign up today, dumbasses. You won't be pitied or missed.

YUTES AND CHIRIN'

We were in the station lot when we heard a school car calling for help. There was an elementary school right down the block from the district station. The school cars took a great deal of work off the backs of the patrol cars. There were only two school units to cover fifteen elementary schools and one high school in the district. Most were public schools. In these schools, because of the age of the students, there was a lot of nonsense that went on daily. Most of it was harmless, but police were there to take the burden off the teachers.

That old expression of "it takes a village to raise a child" did not work well in the 'hood. If a teacher or another parent tried to discipline a child who was not their own, it might result in a conflict that could turn deadly. So, the police had to address many of the kids' behavioral problems before things got out of control.

We ran down the block to help the female officer who was calling for help. As we approached, we saw her trying to control a female student. The female officer was tough and street wise enough to handle most situations. She was working alone and had tried to take a twelve-year-old female student into custody. The student was about five foot seven, weighed a good two hundred fifty pounds, and was actively resisting arrest.

The student had just slashed another girl's throat with a straight razor over a boy she and the victim both liked. It had happened while in the playground. As we ran up and tried to help, we also got caught in the fur ball. Trying to subdue a preadolescent female when you do not want to injure her is problematic. It took six police officers to put this *child* into a shield car.

In another incident, an elementary school had split itself into two opposing groups. One group supported Tupac Shakur and Death Row Records. The other group supported Biggie Smalls, or as he was known in rap circles, "The Notorious B.I.G." Believe it or not, actual fistfights took place in the school regarding this division. It came to our attention when the Tupac faction followed a Biggie supporter home. They pursued the boy to his front door. He ran into his home, and his pursuers kicked in his door to get at him. Fortunately, his mother was home.

His mother stopped the boys and removed them not so gently from her home. The next day, she went to the school to report the boys who had entered her home. We were called. These kids were only nine and ten years old. We had them pulled from class. There were four main offenders.

We did our case report, but instead of taking them in to the station, we called their parents. Some were at work. They were smoking mad when they had to come to school for their children. The kids all received suspensions. They were made to apologize to the woman whose house they had entered. I am pretty sure some parental behavior adjustments would be applied to their nether regions. The teachers took it from there.

These incidents are not uncommon. In most cases, we are witnessing the disintegration of the family unit. In addition, we are also witnessing the increasing dependence on teachers and police to guide children through these formative years. That should be the parents' task, not the police or teachers. We are the guardrails in their journey to adulthood. We should not be the driving force.

＝✦ ✦＝

Another fine summer day, I was in the district station lot looking for my squad car. I saw a school bus pull up on the corner. A knot of kids ran off the bus heading quickly down the block. Some were wearing red T-shirts and were taking them off as they ran. Some were carrying the T-shirts. I thought they might have been on some sort of day-camp excursion.

I was curious enough that I stopped one of the kids carrying a shirt. I asked why he was running while carrying the shirt. He showed it to me. The logo on the front was of a major Chicago street gang. The back of the shirt in two columns had the names of deceased gang members. The street gang had organized an outing for the kids. The reason they were running is that most of our district was the self-proclaimed territory of another major street gang.

With the exception of the block on which the police station sat, the other gang was more predominant. The kids were running because they did not want to be seen by rival gang members. How fucked up is that? The gangs are doing a better job at recruiting youths than the legitimate organizations like the Boy Scouts, Cub Scouts, or Little League.

＝✦ ✦＝

In another incident, I got a call of a domestic disturbance between a brother and sister. I talked to Sis. She was a female gang member with the tattoos to prove it. She and Bro had argued about some stupid shit. She claimed he had hit her. It looked to me that she could have won a fight with an MMA champ. She wanted her brother locked up. I made some quick notes, then had her sign complaints.

I found Sis's brother in the alley working on his car. He denied her allegations. He was a good guy and went along peacefully. While in the station, we got to shooting the breeze. He was worried about his dog, which was tied up in the yard. He told me a story that shocked even my cynical policeman's heart. His dog, a German shepherd, had puppies. Some of the neighborhood kids had begged him for a puppy. He felt bad for them, so he gave them one. They took the puppy down the street, tied it to a tree, then beat it to death with tree branches and rocks.

When the story got back to him, he grabbed one of the little fuckers and asked why. The kid, an eight-year-old, said it was because they had wanted to see what it felt like to kill. If at eight he could kill a defenseless puppy, how do you think he would feel about killing you when he turns sixteen?

The gangs regularly use young kids to kill pit bulls that lose their fights in the pit. They do that to get them used to killing. These young men think of terrible ways to kill wounded animals. I will expand on that later.

⚔︎

It was the end of our watch. My partner and I were working the wagon on days. As we rounded the corner to the station, we saw two fifteen-year-olds beating on another teen. They were giving him a pretty good beating. As I got out of the wagon, one of them gave their victim a downward elbow to the spine. I grabbed that kid. My partner grabbed the other. The teen they were beating shakily stood up. The two idiots said what we had heard many times before: "We just playin'." They said that while giving threatening looks to their victim. I asked the victim if he was hurt. He said no through his bloodied lips. He was clearly afraid of them. I thought, "Fuck it, they are going in."

We put the young thugs in the wagon and drove into the station lot. Those fucks were rocking the wagon back and forth. They were kicking the door and laughing and cursing. I thought, "Wow, if these kids are this bad now, how will they be in four or five years?" But unknown to the idiots, I knew where they lived. I had done a report for Mom. She was tough cookie.

I told my partner to go home; I would handle it. I left the two knuckleheads in the wagon and walked down to Mom's house. I told her what her son and nephew had done to the other boy. I told her how they were acting. I gave her the choice that either she could deal with them, or I would run them through the juvenile justice system. She said that she would deal with them. She was mad. She was scary.

When we walked into the station lot, she could hear them cursing and "acting the fool." I opened the wagon door. The smiles and smirks vanished from their faces, and the laughter died. Now they did not want to get out of the wagon. This lady was fearsome. When she finally got ahold of them, she thanked me.

I had to turn away as she started to use extreme discipline on the both of them all the way down the block. I ran into one of them a few years later. He had done a one-eighty. He was very respectful. He told me he was doing well in school. It might have been a con, but he sounded sincere. Score one for ass-kickin' Mom.

All these incidents occurred within one block of the police station. A few years later, gang members who were on the run shot two officers across the street from the station. One officer was killed, the other crippled by gunfire. I will address that incident later.

The problem with all these incidents, as most will agree, is that these ugly things should not have happened in the first place. They were addressed after the fact. That young girl's throat never should have been slashed. She will bear that scar for life. Those kids never should have been to any function run by gang members. That woman's home never should have been violated. That puppy never should have been tied up then killed. Those two teens never should have beat on another weaker teen. Those police officers never should have been shot. You can't just put these aside as youthful hijinks. Where is the guidance from the families? It is missing.

During my career, whenever I have socially mixed with civilians, I have been asked numerous times, "What do we do to stop the rampant criminal behavior? How would you stop it? What do we do? Can it be stopped?" I mention that in modern times we have had several examples of youth mentored by government.

Dictators recognized that to change a nation, you must shape the youth of the nation. Adolph Hitler created the Hitler Youth. Vladimir Lenin created the All Union Pioneers. Mao Zedong created the Red Guard. Pol Pot created the Khmer Rouge. In each case, they took the youth of their nation and molded them into what they wanted the future of their nations to be. These young minions of the state were responsible for the deaths of millions.

Now it seems the gangs have filled the mentoring vacuum. They teach the kids lack of respect for authority, except their own. They shape the kids into the equals of the above-mentioned state-sanctioned killers. When you are young and taking someone's life, it does not seem unreasonable if you are told to do so by people who have gained your confidence and respect.

We in the United States seem to do nothing to shape our young people into good, productive citizens. They seem to drift through school to, in many cases, a life of dependence on government. Most are unaware of the real history of the United States. They know nothing of the Founding Fathers. They know nothing of the Declaration of Independence, the Constitution, the Bill of Rights, the Revolutionary War, the Civil War, or the Emancipation Proclamation. Just ask them.

What they know about our economic system comes from the drug trade's supply-and-demand model. In the schools, they are socially promoted to their next level of incompetence. Chicago used to be a manufacturing city. The youth were educated to be able to read, write a sentence, do basic math, and speak the language. That was enough for an entry-level job. You took it from there. To succeed or fail was on you. That no longer applies.

I have not been an observer in many classrooms of late. I cannot fault teachers. They many times are bogged down by union rules and government interference. I know they try hard, but they need parental involvement. Otherwise, the only education some of these young people will get is when they visit the prison law library. What's your solution?

WET WORK—THE WAGON

The wagon was a one-ton truck. It sat two officers on a bench seat in the cab. The rest of the truck was a big metal box with a large metal door at the rear. Inside the box were two benches, one on each side. The benches had locked hinged lids, inside the benches was gear necessary to the wagon's function: to transport prisoners, pregnant women, and the dead.

The gear was old and outdated. For the most part, it was unusable. The canvas on the stretcher was dry rotted. The newer stretcher straps were in many cases missing. There was an old rubber body bag that was just plain junk. Most of the usable gear was rusting or not maintained. We had bolt cutters, a sledgehammer, and a pry bar. The purpose of some of the other gear was known but to God.

Over the years, the wagon's configuration changed somewhat, but its purpose did not. Basically, it was a rolling jail. Transporting the dead, I understand is no longer part of its assigned tasks. Also, I do not think it transports pregnant women any longer. That seemed stupid to me at the time, but if a pregnant woman was about to give birth and had no mode of transport or money for a cab, we were assigned to take her to the hospital.

Many of the stories you will read about the wagon in this compilation have to do with the dead. The wagon was called a few different names, one of which was the *paddy wagon*. That name was conferred upon it because of the Irish drunks it transported in Chicago's bad old days. Another name was the *meat wagon*. That name came to use because of the many dead people we hauled. "Meat"—a body devoid of life or soul.

At the time, we took all the dead, regardless of whether it was a natural death or the result of a violent act or accident. As you can guess, the dead were mostly uncooperative in our endeavors to transport them to morgue, hospital, or funeral home. That sometimes led to some gruesomely comedic moments.

Note: If you are easily upset, do not read these next few stories. You will be upset. I guarantee it. You may find our attitudes callous. They were. You cannot deal with corpses on a daily basis and not develop a thick skin. The next six are wagon stories. So, here we go.

THE STUFF OF NIGHTMARES

We spent about an hour going from firehouse to firehouse looking for a disaster bag. At an intersection, we finally located a fire truck soliciting money for the Fireman's Fund for Retarded Children. One firefighter was out in the street with a container shaped like a firefighter's boot. Of course, we had to come up with a couple bucks before we got the disaster bag. It was money well spent.

I was working with a new guy that day. He seemed to be handling it OK. A lot of new guys freaked out when they got a DOA. We pulled up in the alley behind the building. It was three stories with about thirty apartments. My regular partner was standing on the back porch. He was with a new kid too. He stopped by to see if I needed any help.

As I walked up the stairs, I could smell the body already. We walked in to the apartment. It was small, just one room with a bed and a little kitchen. My regular partner had been in there already. He had opened up the windows so the smell wasn't as bad as it could have been plus the open windows cooled the apartment off a bit. Normally, it's so fuckin' hot in some of those apartments that you can barely breathe. It is like you are underwater.

The apartment was dark except for the light coming in from the windows. The only light bulb had died too. That was OK with me. I didn't like looking at their faces. They kind of stay filed away in your mind like some little gallery of horrors.

We looked through the apartment to see if we could find some ID. We found a purse with some pictures and a letter. The body was so decomposed that we couldn't tell if it was this woman or not. The building manager was not there. Some neighbors gave us her name. Needless to say, none of the neighbors wanted to come in to take a look. We decided that there was no foul play involved; she probably just passed from natural causes.

So now it was time to move her. She probably had been lying there for better than a week. Maggots were all over her. She was kind of lying on her side. Well, we had to turn her over to get her in the bag, so I covered her up with a sheet from the bed, then we all put on latex gloves. We laid the bag down next to her, then unzipped it.

All four of us grabbed a part. We began to turn her over. Well, I guess she had built up a little gas because she took a crap right there. One of the new guys dropped his end and ran for the door, gagging. We laughed. We called to him that he would never live it down. Well, the reason it hit him first was that the wind coming in the windows blew the smell right up in his face. When the wind died down, the stink hit the rest of us.

We all headed for the door. I was dry heaving with everybody else on the rear porch. We suddenly started laughing about the whole thing. A bunch of neighbors looking out their windows were shaking their heads. They probably thought we were being irreverent. At that point, we did not much give a fuck. Well, we went back in and finished the job. I had some trouble getting her foot in the bag. That's what I remember most. Her skin just kind of came off on my glove as I stuffed her foot into the bag. We zipped her up and carried her outside, down the stairs, then into the alley. We put her in the wagon.

We stood around and took it easy for a few minutes. We joked around while coming down from the fucking nightmare we had just experienced. It's kind of a copper mental health thing. Humor blunts the horror somewhat. Then we left for the hospital to have her pronounced. The doctor didn't even look at her. He walked out toward the wagon and the smell hit him. He stopped in his tracks, gave us his name and the time pronounced, then walked back into the hospital.

I was out of smokes, so on the way to the morgue, we stopped at a liquor store. I knew the owner. I told him I had locked up one of his underage customers, and the guy was in the back of the wagon calling his name. Before he could go out there, I told him that I was just kidding. I said that we had a stiff in the back that was a little ripe. Well, this guy who was in the store getting a six-pack overheard us talking. He said his father had been in WWII. His dad told him about how bad a dead body smells. He asked if he could see (or smell) for himself. I said, "Sure. Be my guest." The guy went out there and stepped up on the back step of the wagon. The little vent window on the back was open. This guy tried to look in.

Well, I guess he'll believe his dad now because he jumped off the step, dropped his six-pack, then started urping all over the street. He left the six-pack where it lay. He staggered over to his car, vomiting and moaning the whole way. When he finally gained control of himself, he got in his car then drove away. We grabbed the newly abandoned six-pack. No sense wasting perfectly good beer.

Sometimes the God of Moldering Death gives you a little payback for picking up his handiwork. Thank you for the cold beers, God of Moldering Death.

SPAGHETTI?

I was just out of the academy and was working the wagon with one of the old-timers. We got a call to check on a strange odor in an apartment building. I thought, "What the fuck? Do people actually call the police to check on odors?"

The old-timer said, "Aw, shit! We got a 'stinker.'"

We proceeded to the apartment building, and the janitor met us in the hallway. He told us that a guy who lived on the third floor hadn't been seen for a week. We could smell this guy all the way down on the first floor. You know people are curious about death and things pertaining to it. Sometimes I'll tell them a story about a stinker and they'll ask what it smells like. Well, I tell them to imagine taking about one hundred and fifty pounds of raw chicken and putting it in a closed room in the summer, then leaving it in there for about a week. Spoiled meat as most anyone can tell you does not smell like a piney forest. Most people may think they know how bad it can be, but they don't. It is actually worse than they can imagine because of the bodily fluids involved in decomposition. Enough said.

Well, we went up to the apartment with the janitor. He unlocked the door, and before he opened it, we heard kind of a moaning sound. I said, "What the hell is that?" I was getting goose bumps.

The old-timer said, "Flies." We opened the door and were greeted by a veritable blizzard of flies. It's like we walked into "Flies Are Us." You don't want to breathe through your mouth because you might inhale one of them. You know where they have been. So you breathe through your nose. But it stinks like a motherfucker. The smell starts to gag you, so you kind of breathe through your teeth. You speak only when you have to.

It was about eighty degrees outside, but it felt about a hundred in the apartment. Sweat was just pouring off me. Now came the scary part of this whole deal, at least for me. I had never seen a dead body except at a wake and in the military. Now we had to go room to room looking for this dude. I mean, think about it. Hide and seek with a corpse, and you are "It."

After we went through a few rooms, the old-timer spotted the guy on the john. The guy had died taking a dump. I have since learned that this is the way a lot of people go to the great beyond—on the toilet. It's like it's a launching pad to the cosmos or something.

It looked like this guy had been dead about a week. He was sitting there on the bowl and leaning into the wall. His head was melting into the wall. He was a white guy but had turned black from decomposing. He had all this green fungus and shit growing on him and was covered with maggots like grains of white rice crawling all over him.

To my surprise, I was not going to be sick. I guess it was the cool of the old-timer that kept me straight. He treated it as business as usual, like it's a normal, everyday thing to find your worst nightmare dead on a toilet. He told me the smell would have been a lot worse if the guy's back door had not been open to let the place ventilate a little. I could not imagine what worse could be like.

The old-timer took off to go get a body bag from a funeral home. The equipment they give us to work with was shit, so we had to go and beg, borrow, or steal what we needed. When he came back, we went in to get the guy. As you know, most bathrooms are pretty small. Here we had three big guys in this little room. One of us is dead. The old-timer grabbed the guy's shoulders, I grabbed him under the knees, then we heaved him out into the next room and set him down in the bag.

From coming into contact with this guy, I had maggots all over my shoes and pants. So, I start stamping my feet to get them off of me. This resulted in my smashing the maggots as they hit the floor. What fun! Then I pull up my pant legs and brushed them off my socks. More fun!

We zippered this guy up and started taking him down the rear stairway. It was an open stairway, so it was easier to maneuver him around the turns. When we got down to the second-floor landing, an older woman popped out of her door and said, "So, old so-and-so has passed." We said yes, and she said, "I thought something was wrong." We asked why. "Well," she said, "it smelled like he was cooking spaghetti up there for a few days. I had to wonder why would he cook all that spaghetti." The old-timer and I looked at each other and said like in stereo, "Spaghetti?" Hope she is not reviewing restaurants on Yelp. Just sain'.

LAST PUFF

We heard another wagon get a call of a stinker. We knew there were a couple guys working it who weren't regular wagon men. So, we went over to give them a hand. The apartment was in one of those multiunit buildings. It was on the fifth floor. We often wondered if anybody ever died on the first floor. It seemed not so much. So, if you want a long life, live low.

When we got up to the apartment, the two coppers who got the job were just standing there. They were wearing those little masks like they wear in the hospital. You know, the ones that puff out and cover your mouth and nose. I almost burst out laughing because they looked like Pluto, the dog in the Walt Disney cartoons. Their eyes were as big as silver dollars.

It stank in the apartment but was not as bad as it could have been. All the windows were painted shut, but these guys were burning coffee grounds on the stove. It's an old wagon man's trick. You put some coffee grounds in a pan and burn them on the stove. The resulting smell is a little more pleasant than the odor of a rotting body.

I asked where the body was. The "Plutos" pointed to the bathroom. I wanted to laugh again because they looked so funny. I turned away then headed for the john. I found a female corpse. She was a good two hundred pounds at least. Her body was leaning sideways as she sat on the toilet with her head kind of wedged into the corner of the wall. For some reason, it was more decomposed than the rest of her. Her left arm was behind the flush box. She was kind of sliding off the toilet. She probably realized at the last moment that she was dying, stood up, then fell back down in that position.

I grabbed her free arm and tried to pull her upright, but she wouldn't budge. She was wedged in the corner. I noticed everywhere I touched her, the skin was coming off. Blood was oozing to the surface, and she was about ready to burst. I got a strap from the stretcher and tried to get it around her. This was not a pleasant thing to do because my face was inches from her decomposing head.

Finally, I got the strap completely around her middle. I grabbed her left arm from behind the flush box. With my other hand, I gave a good heave on the strap. She started to budge, but then the strap broke. She plopped back down into the corner. I tossed the old, rotted canvas strap and asked the Plutos if they had one of the nylon ones. The two Plutos looked at each other. They didn't know. The only strap they had, came tied around the stretcher.

Finally, my partner went down to get a strap from our wagon. He was not really happy because it was five floors down then five floors up. I was not exactly chuckling myself; it was not even our job. We were only giving an assist to the two Plutos. Again, I went cheek to cheek with Debbie Death. The new strap worked, and I managed to get her off the toilet onto the floor. I walked into the other room and told the two Plutos that it was now all theirs. Their eyes got even bigger.

One of the other coppers who stopped by tore down the shower curtain and spread it on the living room floor so that once we got her out of the bathroom, we could wrap her up. This way she wouldn't leak all over the place while she was being carried down the stairs. Nothing is more unpleasant than being the bottom man on a stiff and having bodily fluids run down onto your uniform.

The two Plutos and I went into the bathroom to drag her out. I had an arm, Pluto one had an arm, and Pluto two was pulling the strap. Well, she was not moving. So we switched to the legs. We all heaved. She started to move. The Pluto pulling on the strap pulled her into an upright position, and she blew a last puff of dead air into his face. He jumped back. I can understand that. Not many people have had the privilege of having a dead person blow in their face. It is the stuff of nightmares.

I imagine at this point he was questioning his commitment to the department. We finally got our gal on the shower curtain and moved her to the stretcher. In the living room, there was more room to work. We tilted her up on her side to get the stretcher under her. Because of lividity, her bottom was a little more decayed than the rest of her—it had been confined by the toilet seat. It resembled kind of a blackened doughnut of ass flesh.

Someone asked how long she had been dead. I saw an opening for some chicanery. Using an old wagon man's trick, I ceremoniously pulled off my purple Nitrile latex gloves and ran my middle finger over her decayed flesh. I licked my index finger. While licking my lips, I said, "About a week, I think." Pluto one ran out the door gagging.

Wagon crews, by necessity, are easily amused. My partner and I had a chuckle at Pluto's expense. He hit the medical and didn't come back for two weeks. Stomach and bowel problems were the reasons given. I am sure his mental health was also a factor. Wagon work is not for everyone.

WE ARE FAMILY II

It was three o'clock in the morning, and I was tired. I didn't feel well. I was working with a woman, and we got a call to check out a strange odor. I knew what that meant. All the way to the address, I was trying to come up with a way out of the call. The female caller met us at the door. She led us up to the fourth floor. As we hit the hallway, I knew what was going on—something was dead.

This lady was like a nut. She kept rambling on nonstop. I felt like telling her to shut the fuck up. We got to the door, which was locked. She told us that her brother lived in there, and she lived right down the hall. She hadn't seen him for a week. All of a sudden, after a week went by, she got worried about this guy at three o'clock in the morning and called the police. Just my luck. I told her some legal mumbo jumbo about us having no right to force open this guy's door. I told her to wait until morning, call the building manager, then get a key. We left.

The woman I was working with said, "Why did you do that?" I didn't answer. I was really just not in the mood to handle a decomposing body on this particular night. Twenty minutes later, we got the call again. Now I was fuckin' mad. When we got there, this nitwit woman had gained entry to the apartment. She had called the janitor of the building at home and had him come and open the door. I wanted to choke her.

We went into the apartment. This guy was just fuckin' goo. He had maggots all over him. He was naked and lying sideways on the bed on his back. His head was hanging over the edge of the bed, and his throat was split wide open from the weight of his head hanging down. The maggots were having a feast. I was hoping the female officer I was with was happy now. Meanwhile, the goofy bitch who called us was over poking at the corpse. I mean, she was patting this guy on the head, and his hair was falling out into a pile on the floor.

A couple other coppers came by. They volunteered to try to get us a body bag. I could have kissed them. This guy was definitely too gooey for a stretcher. While we were waiting, this crazy lady started cleaning out the guy's apartment. I don't mean cleaning up, I mean cleaning out. She started wheeling out the guy's rack stereo. I said, "Hey! What are you doing?" She told me that her brother said she could have the stereo for a party she was giving the next night.

Then came the dawn. I had to bite my tongue lest I say something inappropriate. I smiled a sinister wagon-man smile, A smile like a crocodile. She did not smile back.

<u>GREEN</u>

We got a call of a DOA at the YMCA. Of course, this guy was on the fourth floor. We went into the apartment, if you can call a room smaller than a jail cell an apartment. The guy was sitting in one of those wing-back chairs with the arm rests. He was green. He had been dead a few days. He stank. His eyes were closed, and under the lids, they were swollen to the size of golf balls. He had long hair down to his shoulders. He looked like a Martian biker—kind of like something you would see in *MAD Magazine*.

We closed the door to the hallway to keep the curious away. We started going through this guy's things to determine who he was and who his next of kin might be. My partner found an old, heavy suitcase in the closet. We both thought, "Could this be the mother lode?" Every copper's dream is to find the equivalent of a D. B. Cooper dead plus a couple million in a suitcase. As it turned out, it was only some overdue library books. The only money this guy had were some pennies stuffed into Pall Mall cigarette packages. The packs of pennies were arranged very neatly in the top drawer of his dresser.

After a while, we found the name of a relative and gave him a call. It was this guy's nephew who had not seen him in ten years. The nephew definitely did not want to spend any money to take care of old Uncle Martian's burial. He called all over the city. He finally found a place that would cremate the guy and then dispose of the ashes for $250. A real nice send-off. I guess like the frog says, "It's not easy being green."

My partner was bottom man on the stretcher. This was not a wonderful place to be when carrying a ripening corpse. This guy's Martian fluids were running down into the sleeve of my partner's jacket. I'm sure his dry cleaner would not be very pleased with that garment. We slid the guy in the back of the truck. My partner had to go back in the Y to clean up. An errant thought popped into my head. "YMCA" stands for the "Young Men's Christian Association."

I had never seen a young man in the place. Everybody in there seemed to be old and dying, like a waiting room to the afterlife. Take a number. Wait your turn. Next. Uncle Martian's number was up.

We get permission to take this guy to a south-side funeral home. The funeral director was black, we were white, and Uncle Martian was green. We looked like a Benneton ad. I did not think the funeral director was expecting Uncle Martian to be in the condition he was in. But, $250 is $250. We said our good-byes. We would not soon forget Uncle Martian, especially since the odor of my partner's jacket kept bringing back fond memories of our brief association. Sometimes it's not easy being blue.

<u>OOPS!</u> I

We get a call of a stiff in a house. When we get there, the guy's whole family was there—sons, daughters, brothers, sisters, uncles, aunts, cousins, and for good measure, a couple friends and neighbors. Everybody was sniffling and crying or talking in low whispers. You could tell we were not very welcome. I'm sure they would have rather had a funeral home or an ambulance take their beloved from his home.

We try to be as tactful as we can when asking pertinent questions of the grieving family members. We explained that since he was a relatively young man with no history of medical problems that he had to be taken to the medical examiner's office to determine his cause of death. We filled out our report. You could see that we were starting to win them over with our professional attitude.

When we finally had everybody calmed down, we got down to the nitty-gritty of moving this guy. The trouble was that we had only one strap to hold him on the stretcher. I closed the door to the bedroom so as not to offend the sensibilities of the family. We got the guy on the stretcher and wrapped him in his bed sheet. We really cranked the strap tight so he wouldn't move on us. I opened the door. My partner cleared a path through the crowd. I started wheeling the guy through his living room using the little set of wheels at the head of the stretcher. He was head down so that when we lifted him into the wagon, he would go in headfirst and we would just roll him in.

Everything was going just fine until we tried to get the stretcher into the front hall, which was very narrow. It was a really tight turn. I lifted up on the handles and stood this guy almost straight up. That's when the strap gave. The guy shot out from the sheet headfirst into the crowded living room. There were a lot of shocked, open-mouthed gasps along with some angry glares—a real Kodak moment. All I could think to say was, "OOPS!"

Getting this stiff back on the stretcher then out the door in the now total silence of the living room was about as much fun as a prostate exam. We felt all alone like a chicken bone. We were, however, nominated to the "wagon man's hall of infamy" by the personnel working the other two squadrols. Their hyena-like yowling was the end of a not-so-perfect day!

THE END OF WET WORK

ANOTHER TWOFER

I was writing parking tickets on a block where parking was a problem. The people in the neighborhood had complained at a community beat meeting that people were leaving unlicensed cars on the street for long periods of time. They took issue with neighborhood entrepreneurs starting up curbside car washes. Also, alley parkers were a problem. Some residents could not pull into their own garages because they were blocked by illegally parked cars.

When I was not on a call, I was writing parking tickets on the blocks that were having problems. There were plenty of violators, so I had no problem filling the time between calls. Most of the streets in this area were residential, one-family homes with a sprinkling of apartment buildings. Generally, these streets were quieter than most. There was a drug trade, but it was not as open and notorious as on other corners.

The residents had requested that their streets be blocked off to prevent drug-trade vehicle traffic. So many of the blocks were not accessible from the main street. That worked to some extent, but the dealers were quick to adapt. They moved their operations to the other side of the barriers that blocked the streets. Now the police were also blocked during vehicle and foot pursuits.

If a drug seller ran from us, a car could not pursue without going all the way around the barrier through the alleys. Also, our response to calls suffered because of the tortuous routes we had to take to get to an in-progress call. So far, there was no permanent solution to the problem.

On that particular day, I saw a parked vehicle with a bogus "applied for" paper sticker in the window. At that point in time, when you applied for a license, you were given a paper receipt to post in your rear window until your plates arrived in the mail. The sticker showed that you had applied for plates. This was a very stupid system. Every numbskull immediately figured out how to mimic the receipt. A third grader could do it.

The wrongdoers knew we could not read the piece of paper from a distance or see if it was legit unless we were right on it. As I wrote a ticket for a fake sticker, I noticed the name on the sticker. It was a car thief I had arrested in the past. I ran the VIN (vehicle identification number), and it came back a steal. I thought, "What the fuck? Why would this guy, who is a known auto thief, put his real name on a bogus sticker?" It could be that if he was pulled over, he was counting on the fact that the info on his fake sticker matched the name on his license, and possibly the police would not check his VIN.

Whatever his criminal motivation, I was going to lock him up again. I knew he was a police fighter from previous experience. He generally would not go easy. The address on the sticker was across the street. I asked for an assist. They were on the way. I asked an elderly man nearby if he knew who parked the car. "Yes," he answered. "He lives over there," pointing across the street. "He just parked maybe a half hour ago." I wanted to make sure the address on the sticker was the correct address and not some criminal dodge.

I felt the hood of the car. It was still warm. My assist arrived, and we went across the street. The guy's name was on the second-floor mailbox. We went up to the apartment and knocked. He opened the door. I asked his name. He gave me a bogus name. He evidently did not remember that I had locked him up before. I was hurt and disappointed. I asked for his ID, and he asked why. I made up some bullshit about looking for "Joe Schmo" on a warrant. He produced his license. His ID matched the sticker. He must have forgotten his real name as it differed from the one he just gave us. Very sad.

We would give him a place to think and remember his real name. We were well known for our citywide think tanks. I told him he was under arrest for auto theft. He looked like he was sizing us up for a fight. He made the right decision and turned around. We cuffed then searched him. As we were coming down the stairs, I monitored a call with a description of a strong-arm robbery offender from an adjoining suburb.

Evidently, one of our miscreants had crossed over the line separating Chicago from a more affluent suburb. He had accosted a thirteen-year-old and smashed him in the face, possibly breaking his nose. He then took the young teen's very expensive ten-speed bicycle. Dispatch gave a pretty good physical and clothing description. The bike was a bright-blue ten-speed.

As we took our auto thief down the front stairs, we found a crowd had gathered to see the police activity. It seemed like no matter what the time of day it was, a crowd always materialized. Street zombies. But in this case, it was a good thing because, you guessed it. "Dummy Bike Thief," the felonious thug, was among the street zombies. He had stopped to see what we were doing on his brand-new, bright-blue, ten-speed bicycle.

I yelled out to a unit near him to grab him. Dummy Bike Thief froze like a deer in headlights. By the time he figured shit out, he was in hand. We called the zone to tell them to have the suburban cops slide by. They came by with their bloody victim. The victim ID'd Dummy Bike Thief and the bike. Dummy Bike Thief would be charged with strong-arm robbery.

We took Dummy Bike Thief and Dummy Car Thief into our think tank. We did the paperwork to turn Dummy Bike Thief over to the suburban coppers. They had a think tank too. We cleared two crimes. We took two bad guys off the street. It was a good day for the workin' police.

DOGS

Note: Again, if you are a sensitive soul, <u>do not</u> read this.

Dogs have been our companions since the wolf formed a hunting bond with our prehistoric ancestors. They helped us hunt prey. We took them into our campfire's circle of light. They have been our faithful friends ever since.

I think dogs are the only animals that would die to save us. They have in all our wars accompanied our soldiers into battle. They are in our airports as bomb-sniffing dogs. They are at our borders to detect illegal border crossings. Dogs are used to detect firearms and narcotics. They lead the blind, they comfort the afflicted, they teach responsibility and care to children. All they want in return is a pat on the head and a word of praise. They are in many cases better than most people. They are not duplicitous, they will not betray you, and their love is unconditional. Black, white, rich, poor—they do not care. They are loyal until death.

In America, dogs have become family members. We have repaid them in most cases with love and care until their sad ends.

Not so in the 'hood. Staffordshire bull terriers or "Pit Bulls" are the dogs that are most mistreated by the idiots I have dealt with. From birth, the animals are mistreated. If one is born that appears weak, it is killed. Many times, the mothers of dogs losing a fight are killed.

These dogs are raised in an ugly environment by people who fight them to make money. Their training is as primitive as the people who raise them. I have seen them with weights hanging from chains around their necks. In some cases, they wear a kind of jacket with weights in it. This is to make them strong for fighting. They are fed all kinds of crazy diets by these nitwits. They are usually confined in stand-up positions so they cannot move, turn, or lie down.

Keep in mind that the dogs know no other kind of life or any kind of love. The dogs try to please their monstrous owners. The owners train the dogs to kill by encouraging them to kill captive cats or other small animals like rabbits. They are starved until killing becomes normal behavior.

Stray dogs in the 'hood and dogs taken from yards or from their owners are used as bait. The bait dogs have their mouths wired shut or their teeth ground down to the gums so they cannot fight back or protect themselves. If a pit bull will not kill or maim its opponent, it is killed. If it becomes maimed or loses a fight, it is killed. A famous NFL quarterback killed dogs that lost fights by lifting them over his head and then smashing their heads on the pavement. He also drowned and hung dogs. He fed his own pet dogs to the pits for a laugh. He went to prison for his monstrous behavior.

In the 'hood, the dogfights are run by the street gangs. If a dog is badly mauled, it may be given to the younger gang members to dispose of. This is their first taste of killing. These kids may be as young as eight years old. I myself have seen the following. I saw a sack lying in the street in an industrial area. The sack contained the bodies of three young pit bulls that had been skinned. They had also been run over by cars multiple times. I found a pit bull under a tree near a grade school. It was still alive after having been set afire. Three pit bulls were found leashed to a railroad track just before they were to be hit by a train.

Unfortunately, all pit bulls taken to the pound in Chicago are immediately euthanized. It is thought most will never be fit for adoption because of their training and mistreatment. I do not agree but I am not the mayor. I once found a dog in an open field. He was in an improvised doghouse that was just big enough for him to stand in; otherwise, he could not move. Sharp nails were driven into the interior from the outside so that if the animal moved in any direction, he would be stuck by a nail. Unfortunately, that dog was also euthanized. After a life of pain, his reward was death.

The pits are also used for protection. Gang members may transport money or dope, but instead of carrying a gun, they will have a pit bull on a leash. If I had to stop someone with a pit, I would tell them to tie the dog to a fence or pole. I told them right out that if they released the Pit on me, I would kill them first, then the dog. A Pit Bull can kill or seriously maim a person. Thankfully, nobody tested me by releasing their dog.

Many times, dope houses, where they process and package dope for the street, have Pits to ward off or delay intrusion by police or rival gangs. These dogs are killed on police entry. If they live, they are euthanized. In my opinion, they are euthanizing the wrong animals. Ironically, the same people who torture these animals call each other "Dog." They do not deserve the name.

Most of these dog torturers will themselves wind up in small cages from which they cannot escape (prison). Some of them will also be killed in inhumane ways (shanked). In the Tao of the street, justice will be done. The New Testament states that the wage of sin is death. Your paycheck is on the way, dog killers. Rightly so.

EXPEDIANTLY EXPENDABLE

It was early fall. The sun was shining and all creatures great and small seemed in order. Then, in a district not our own, a problem was beginning. It seems that in a factory that made plating chemicals, a fire was about to start. In the factory were toxic chemicals that when heated turned into a toxic gas.

As in many parts of the old city of Chicago, the factory was in a residential neighborhood. Not good. As the fire got going, the fire department had protocols for dealing with the deadly gas that could be emanating from the fire. According to wind direction and toxicity, the firefighters determined the area directly north of the fire had to be evacuated. That area comprised a three-block-by-three-block grid or nine square blocks.

The district the fire was in was one of the busiest in the city. Its manpower, like ours, was always stretched to its breaking point. It did not have enough people to respond to calls, cordon off the area, then evacuate nine square blocks. Their field lieutenant called our watch commander to request some manpower. Our watch commander said he would send his foot patrols and school cars to help in the evacuation. So, off we went.

When we got to the location, all five of us were sent down the blocks. We were to go door to door to ask the people to leave their homes as there was a danger of toxic gas emanating from the fire. We all did our jobs as quickly as we could. The guys from the district we were helping sat in their patrol cars watching us. Finally, when I got to the end of the block closest to the fire, I ran into a problem. I was two houses away from the rear of the burning factory. I think the fire department was close to getting the upper hand on the fire as there was more smoke than fire.

In the second house from the rear of the burning building was a man who was an immobile heart patient. I told him he would have to leave, and I would get an ambulance to move him. He agreed. I got on the radio to request an ambulance, then went to the last house on the block. After notifying that resident to evacuate, I went back to the elderly heart patient. I got on the radio again and asked for an ambulance. I could see the ambulance sitting three blocks down. It was not moving. I asked the zone what was going on as I could see the ambulance from my location. I was told they were not coming. I asked why not. I thought there was some CFD protocol they had to deal with or they needed a supervisor's permission. I was then told that the area I was in was too toxic for them to enter to transport the elderly heart patient. I then asked the zone, "Then why the fuck are you sending us down here if it is too dangerous for the paramedics?" Silence. I was pissed.

They had used us when they knew that shit was toxic. I blamed their lieutenant. He knew. He sent us instead of his guys. He might possibly have sent a car with a public-address system to get those people out or used some other method. But that would have taken thought. Why would you do that thinking stuff when you had street grunts to do the work? After all, that is what the worker bees are for. Sacrifice them for the greater good. Put yourself in for a medal, lieutenant.

I got the elderly man into a wheelchair, then wheeled him for three blocks. Shortly thereafter the fire was struck. When we got back to the district, I filed a complaint with the FOP against the lieutenant for sending us into that shit when he knew the fumes were toxic. We all had some irritant-related breathing problems, but after a few days, they thankfully passed.

Of course, filing a complaint on a boss is just not good form for the lowly ground pounders. Guess what? The complaint went nowhere. I guess that was because we did not all die.

PIZZA PIZZA OR DUM FUCKERY REDUX

A new family with two young kids moved into the neighborhood. They came in from a high-crime neighborhood. Usually, parents move to a better neighborhood from a worse neighborhood to give their kids a shot at staying alive and out of gangs. They do it to keep the kids away from the thug life. But even with the best intentions, sometimes parents will be thwarted by their children's dum fuckery.

On this particular night, Moms was at work, Pops had been elsewhere for a long time. Her children Tweedle Dee and Tweedle Dummy were getting bored. They were ten and eleven years old. You may ask yourself what could a ten- and eleven-year-old do that would be so bad they could go to jail? If you answered yourself by saying, "Self, How about armed robbery? Alex for sixty dollars." Ding Ding Ding. You are correct, Kreskin. Stand in line for your Junior Colombo decoder ring.

Yes, the Tweedle brothers have concocted a plan where they will get some "dead president" spending cash and eat at the same time. They will rob the pizza delivery man. They had a look alike plastic gun. It was the kind of plastic gun that would get you shot if you upped it on the police.

They called in for two pizzas, one pizza for each brother. They hid across the street to ambush the driver as he exited the car. They waited. About half an hour went by. Then they saw the deliveryman's car turn the corner. They rushed the deliveryman as he exited the car with the pizzas.

Tweedle Dee stuck the plastic gun in his face while Tweedle Dummy took the pizzas then went through the pizza deliveryman's pants and took his wallet and pizza money. The Tweedle brothers then forced the frightened pizza deliveryman into the trunk of his car. They slammed the trunk shut. Success was theirs. They took the pizzas and the cash and went home. They laughed. They giggled. They ate the pizzas. They fell asleep.

The pizza deliveryman was very frightened. He waited awhile, then began to bang on the trunk lid hoping someone would hear him. After some time, a citizen walking by heard him banging on the trunk lid and called police. When the police arrived, they punched the trunk lock and freed the driver. They listened as the pizza man told them what had happened. The police asked for the address he was dispatched to.

The police started at square one to determine if the people at the address knew the offenders. Well, guess what, Junior G-Men? When the police knocked on the door, Tweedle Dummy opened it. The police could see the empty pizza boxes on the floor of the living room. They snatched up Tweedle Dummy then woke up Tweedle Dee.

On the floor with the pizza boxes was the money, the plastic gun, and the deliveryman's wallet. The deliveryman ID'd the Tweedles. The master criminals had given their own address to the deliveryman's employer. Even the Gods of Dum Fuckery were ashamed of the Tweedles.

Their ordeal was just beginning. No more giggling and laughing would they be "a doin". They were on their way to be processed by the Kiddy Cops. Soon after, the Tweedles would be dealing with a very angry Mama Tweedle. Not a good thing for Tweedle Dee and Tweedle Dummy. They would be eating their meals while standing up for a while. Noim sain.

THE GREAT TRAIN ROBBERY

During the era after the Civil War, America became a somewhat lawless society. You cannot send thousands of young men to fight in a war and not have a few survivors bear some anger and bitterness over having lost. Thus, you had Jesse James and the James-Dalton Gang. Train robbers and bank robbers. They would stop trains by a variety of means or board trains as passengers with the intent of robbery. They would rob the mail car, which usually contained payrolls and other valuables. While they had some early successes, most of the gang members eventually came to a bad end.

Of course, the modern-day train robbers we dealt with were as dense as fucking uranium. This is a story of some sub-primordial dunces who engaged in their emulations of the legendary train robbers of the past. They would make a Faustian deal with the devil. Whereas they would give up playing Jordan vs. Bird - One on One from their raggedy ass couch, to gain whatever was in Boxcar #1.

In our district, the El tracks ran East to West. Parallel to the El tracks were railroad tracks. For whatever reason, many of these freight trains stopped in our district. They would not move for hours. Our train-spotting crew had been waiting for this opportunity. They assembled their version of the Wild Bunch. The Befuddled Bunch. These eight to ten thugs came up with a plan to climb a two-story embankment, break into a boxcar, then form a human chain to offload the loot to ground level where they would then abscond with said loot. They quickly put their plan into action. They climbed the two-story embankment. They used an assortment of crowbars and screwdrivers to break into a boxcar. They formed a human chain to offload their loot—TVs, microwaves, stereo systems with speakers—oh my!

The boxes they took had a big, long, foreign-sounding name on them. Must be some good shit. Done stacking as many of the boxes as they all could carry, they set off down the street. In his haste to get away, one of them tripped on a crack in one of the city's unrepaired sidewalks. The box fell to the ground. It split open. No one heard this, but we can speculate what was said: "Aw, fuck, man—books." Our heroes had stolen eight heavy boxes of the *Encyclopedia Britannica*. We found those boxes after a call by a citizen the next day. They lay at intervals on the broken sidewalk leading back to the boxcar. No one in the high-crime neighborhood took even one book. Shocking!

NURSES

In a police officer's little corner of the world, several synergistic occupations exist. These include judges, lawyers of all sorts, Chicago firefighters and paramedics, waitresses, bartenders, doctors, and nurses. Of course, not ranked in that order.

As a police officer, you spend a great deal of time in hospitals. The nurses are the backbone of the hospital staff. It was they who carried the physical and mental burden of the work that needed to be done. We brought them loads of very unpleasant people to care for. Also, they were ofttimes burdened with the victims of our very unpleasant people. To their credit, they took care of both with the same professionalism.

Most times, needless to say, we were not too concerned with the bad guy's condition. We did not wish them well or that they would have any modicum of longevity. But nurses always did their best. Most of them were about as burned out as we were, but they knew they did not sign up for ballroom-dancing classes. This was the job.

To cite only a few examples to illustrate their dedication does not really do them justice. But, here they are. This was our everyday reality. We brought in a homeless man who probably had had no medical care for many a moon. It had been a cool fall day when we spotted him shaking violently. We called for a wagon for a transport and brought him into the ER. We signed him in with what info we had.

To its credit, the hospital never turned anyone away. Because of this, it was going broke. The nurses had to strip off the homeless man's clothing. That was no cup of tea. He was filthy. His clothing was filthy. His clothes were so thread bare that they were starting to disintegrate. They removed his clothes as gently as they could. When it came to his socks, they had not been removed for so long that they were actually embedded into the skin at the bottom of his feet.

They got him cleaned up and prepped for the doctor to examine. They gave him some water to sip on until the doctor had a chance for diagnosis. God bless them for doing what even the most compassionate among us would have second thoughts about doing. Whether it was Warren Buffett, Michael Bloomberg, or our guy "Joe Nobody," they all got the same first-rate care.

On another occasion, I was coming into the emergency room to finish a report in the hospital's police room. As I was entering, I observed a nurse trying to assist a pregnant woman. She was trying to get the woman up onto a gurney so she could be wheeled into the hospital. The woman's water had already broken, and she was really close to giving birth.

As I stood back to give them some room, the woman put one leg up onto the gurney. At that point, the baby shot out from her vagina like a cannonball. The nurse caught the baby like a line drive to the shortstop. In reality, it was like catching a greased turkey. The umbilical cord was still attached. The rest of the bloody goo came shortly after. She handed the baby to the mother, helped her up onto the gurney, then wheeled her into the ER.

I was fucking amazed. I am still amazed. I asked the nurse later if things like that happened often. She told me that it mostly happened with mothers addicted to crack cocaine.

On another occasion, I was assigned to guard a prisoner in the hospital. He had swallowed twenty bags of rock that had been left unattended when a tac officer went to get an inventory book. The officer had left the twenty bags of crack cocaine within reach of the long-armed criminal. This guy was taken to the hospital because if any of those bags broke in his stomach, it might kill him. If they wanted me to get the evidence when he took a crap, they had sent the wrong guy.

This guy had more than a few charges. I had to guard him until relieved by the Cook County sheriff's officer. When a doctor gave the OK, this guy would be headed to the county jail. When I relieved the other officer guarding this mutt, he took his cuffs off the guy and I put mine on. He was cuffed to the hospital bed. I had also brought along my leg cuffs. An old-timer gave them to me when he retired. They had come in handy more than once with extremely violent bad guys or off-the-chart mental patients.

The hospital could not clear this guy until he took a crap. I hoped he would wait until the county officer got there. It was not to be. This mutt asked to use the facilities. I uncuffed him from the bed but left the leg cuffs on. On his way to the john, he grabbed on to a sink. He looked very sick. From his overloaded colon, his sphincter released a two-foot stream of black shit. It dribbled to a cow-pie-like pile on the shiny hospital floor and on my shiny leg cuffs. Yikes! Just as I was about to say something very uncharitable, a floor nurse came in the ward space we were in. She grabbed some towels and started cleaning up the crap. She was not mad or miffed. She acted like it was an everyday thing.

I considered the place I was in. I was in a hospital full of sick people. The nurses had to deal with the same crap in the hospital that we dealt with outside, except ours was more about behavior than actual feces. It was part of the job. The nurse wiped off my leg cuffs. When I cuffed my prisoner to the bed, I took off the leg cuffs. The nurse soaked them in some kind of green germ-killing liquid, then gave them back. I was very grateful. She just shrugged it off with a little smile, then went to look in on another patient.

This is what nurses do, God bless them. Consider that when someone with no family or loved ones passes over to the other side, usually the last face he or she will see will be one of these angels wearing scrubs. Thanks, angels.

A BUCK FIFTY

One of the guys was on furlough, and we were way down on manpower. I was working a foot patrol. I got pulled off the foot patrol to take another officer's beat until he came back. I had worked this beat before—it was not the best but also was not the worst.

The only real problem on the beat was a small group of "gangstas." They were young, but some serious criminal acts had been perpetrated by their little gang. That included murder. In one case, a witness to a shooting had done the right thing by giving information to the police. They put a couple shotgun blasts through the witness's back door. The witness stopped his cooperation with the police. He moved from the neighborhood the next day, and his house went up for sale within the week.

I had been dispatched on a men-selling-drugs call, and while in the area, I stopped a teen who fit the description of one of the wrongdoers. He was only fifteen. He gave me some attitude during a pat-down search for weapons. He went for disorderly conduct. When I asked when was the last time he had been in custody, he told me he had just beat a murder charge. I found out later in speaking with a youth officer that yet again, the witness or witnesses had been threatened and then refused cooperation.

During an eight-hour tour, the department wanted us to do two fifteen- to twenty-minute foot patrols. Most times we were so busy that this task was not doable. When there was some time to do a foot patrol, most officers remained in their cars. Experience had taught us that another of *Officer Einstein's Laws of Police Work* would kick in. It was common that dispatch routinely pulled officers off foot patrol and sent us wherever they thought there was a more pressing problem. The seriousness of the call dispatched was directly associated with how far you were from your vehicle. One of *Officer Einstein's Rules of Time and Space* stated: *"The farther you are from your vehicle, the more serious the call to which you will be dispatched."* Consequently, a learned behavior was to sit in your car and observe the street rather than take a stroll and then have to hurry back to respond to in-progress calls, where time was of the essence.

I knew the several spots these young gangstas congregated. So, I went down on my foot patrols at those locations. I would get out of the car. I would stand among them. That kind of put a stick in their spokes. After doing that numerous times, I learned most of their names and approximate addresses. We would shoot the shit for twenty minutes or so, then I would go back to motorized patrol. So, for twenty to forty minutes a day, the good people in the neighborhood caught a break.

In speaking with these young guys, I learned that most felt they could not get out of the life they had chosen. They felt tied to the 'hood. I suggested a radical concept. Walk two blocks. Get on a bus. Pay a buck fifty. Go somewhere else. What? I suggested there was a whole city out there seven miles wide and twenty-seven miles long. For a buck and a half, you could be somewhere else. A ball game, a museum, a movie, or a pizza place were options.

I saw a couple neurons firing among the group. However, I did not expect any "road to Damascus" epiphanies. I was not disappointed. About a month later, as I was signing out a new ticket book, I glanced over at the juvenile detention cage and saw some familiar faces. They were laughing and clowning, much to the consternation of the desk mice, who resented that their search for lunch menus was being interrupted.

I went over to the cage. The young gangstas were unrepentant about their latest criminal behavior of selling drugs by a school. We exchanged pleasantries. They were now at the first stop on the express train to "three hots and a cot." The last stop would be in one of the big, gray-walled, state-supported institutions. Clear the tracks. ALL ABOARD.

WHORES

W hores are everywhere in Chicago. Shocked that there are whores in the city? Don't be. There have been whores here since there has been a city on this spot. In fact, there are whores in every city in the United States and the world. You may think there are no whores in your more-wealthy neighborhoods. You are wrong. They are there. They just wear better clothes, and they don't stand in the street. But they are there.

The whores we encountered in our district were a mix of white, black, and Latina. The majority were black because we worked in a majority black district. The whores are a cross section of America. I am sure as little girls they never in a million years thought they would be doing what they were doing. We generally did not give them a *60 Minutes* interview when we stopped them. So, in most cases, we did not have any idea why a particular girl or guy was out there selling sexual favors. But, every once in a while, we got some insight.

There was one girl whose street name was Paradise. She was attractive and well spoken. So, I asked what every copper since the beginning of time has asked girls who had looks plus intellect going for them. "Why in the fuck are you doing this?" Here is the story she told me.

She had been fifteen years old and was dating a guy who was twenty-one. Her grandmother had told her to be home at ten o'clock. As usual, we again see the grandmother raising the children of some narcotics-addicted mother with no father the child would ever know. I wonder if that may have been a factor? Hmm.

Paradise got to her front door at 2:00 a.m. Her boyfriend was waiting in the car until she was safely in the house. What a gentleman. When Paradise looked through her front window, she saw Grandma with a folded-up extension cord (a common disciplinary tool in the 'hood) waiting for her. She could choose to go in and receive a beating or go with the boyfriend. She told me she made the wrong choice. She wished in retrospect that she had chosen to take the beating.

The boyfriend got her hooked on heroin and then turned her out. Money was taken as fast as she made it. There were no whore savings accounts. If she held cash back, her pimp would beat her. She was also at risk of getting a life-ending STD.

After a while, I never saw her again. I hope she made it out of that life, but I am afraid most of the whores get out only through death from overdose (sometimes intentional), an STD, or a beating from a trick or a pimp that went too far. Not a happy ending.

Another story that comes to mind is of a woman who was drop-dead gorgeous when you saw her from a half block away. In the sodium-vapor lights of evening, she looked like a cross between all the sex symbols of the '70s and '80s. However, when you got close up, you could see the ravages of heroin addiction and AIDS. Those two maladies usually traveled hand in hand.

She usually wore long sleeves because of the ulcerated track marks on her arms. After constant use, the veins eventually collapse, causing the addict to seek other veins. Her injection sites were infected, possibly from immune-system collapse. Addicts wind up shooting up anywhere they can still find a vein.

This woman had started to use the veins in her face. Those sites were also ulcerated. She used makeup as thick as plaster to cover them up. In the light, she was horrifying. She also had gotten awfully thin. Frankly, it looked like she did not have much time left. She told me she lived by herself, that she did not have a pimp. I believed her.

Working the wagon one night, we turned on to the main drag where prostitutes plied their trade. It was about two in the morning. We observed a woman talking through the open passenger window of a stopped auto. As we approached, the talking stopped, then the vehicle drove off. The lady standing on the corner at the bus stop looked like she did not belong there. She lacked the whore mode of dress and looked like a housewife/mother. We stopped to inquire what she was doing there and also asked about the nature of her conversation with the occupant of the vehicle that had pulled away. We got the old "he was asking for directions" dodge.

We said that we could put her in the wagon, catch up with the guy, and ask him what he had said. Did she think he would say the same thing? She knew we had her. She then admitted that she was out trying to make a little money to feed her children. She told us that her husband had left her. She had no money to feed the kids. She had nothing. We told her we would not arrest her but we did not want to see her again. We told her where she could get some help during the day from social services. We then each ponied up some cash for the kids. Chumps? Maybe. We never did see her again. Money well spent!

Many people will say that if women or men are out there whoring, why don't we arrest them? The simple answer is that to arrest them for prostitution, we have to observe the actual sexual act, then prove that money was paid for the sex. This is not practical or doable. For the most part, unless you can walk into a motel room with probable cause while the act is being performed, then see money paid for services rendered, they cannot be arrested. You will agree this is not practical.

Arrests can be made for soliciting money for sex or interfering with the orderly flow of traffic. In a district with a high incidence of violent street crime, that also is impractical. So, for the most part, we live and let live or die as the case may be.

A LOVELY MAN

When my friend first came to the district, he was assigned to work with one of our most preeminent burnouts. Officer Burnout was an expert at hanging back on jobs. When he was assigned an in-progress job, he hung back just enough so someone else would get to that job first. If it was no big deal, he would code it out. If it was an arrest situation, he would ask that the job be reassigned to the unit that made the arrest.

Officer Burnout's basic excuse, like other burnouts, was that he had spent time in an elite, specialized gang unit. These officers posited that they had accomplished in five years what us lowly street grunts could not do in twenty. During that assignment, they had burned out. They were done working. For the next fifteen or twenty years, they would just be collecting a paycheck.

The thing they did not say is why they got dumped from those elite units and put into our district. It was a shame because on the few occasions Officer Burnout did choose to work, he was very good. But those occasions were few and far between.

My friend was initially assigned to work with Officer Burnout. Most new officers, after training with an FTO is over, are many times put with the guys nobody wants to work with. After a while, most of us do find someone we like to work with and then make that transition—that is, if the bosses allow it.

Unfortunately, my friend got a poor reputation by association because he worked with Officer Burnout. One fine day, I was partnered with him. I thought, "Fuck. I have to work with this do-nothing copper?" I was pleasantly surprised. We got a job of a rape in progress in the garage. We slid down the alley as quietly as we could so as not to spook the rape offender.

As we hit the address, a man ran from the garage. My friend was on him like a hawk on a rabbit. The offender was big. He was about six foot two and about 250 pounds. My friend was also big. He was a tough Irish kid who could handle himself. My friend had the suspect cuffed before I could put the wagon in park. I was fucking impressed. Just then, the victim staggered up from the floor at the rear of the abandoned garage. She was in her mid-twenties. Her clothing was torn and dirty, and her face was puffy from the beating she had received. We called for an ambulance. We gave a field interview to the arrestee, who was sixteen. He was as close a throwback to a pre-Homo erectus hominid as you could possibly get without time travel. He had a bad complexion, his head came to a point, plus when you looked into his eyes, there were no lights on and nobody home.

He told us she was a "ho" who had agreed to "give him some." When she did not "give him some," he exclaimed he would not pay her. Hence, the argument that resulted in her beating. A custodial search proved he had no money to pay her, even if he were telling the truth. We put him in the wagon to ruminate on when next he could pick fruit pits from elephant dung.

Her story was that she was a whore but she was not working. She was walking down the alley to the corner store. He jumped out from the garage, pulled her in, then tried to rape her. She started screaming, then someone called the police. We felt she was telling the truth. She was not dressed in her whore uniform, it was ten o'clock in the morning, and she didn't live far from the garage.

We knew then, though, that this was going nowhere. We believed her, but a public defender would easily impeach her testimony when her rap sheet was pulled. It would be just enough to establish reasonable doubt. But we would give it a shot. If nothing else, we had him on battery and unlawful restraint.

As an added bonus, we could fill out a school absentee card, which would give our stats-oriented bosses an instant boner. Fuck all the rest of that "policey" crap. A school absentee was proof positive we were striking back at those young criminal miscreants. Yes, we were. The suspect was not in school, which was a very serious crime worthy of upper-echelon accolades. Well, as we thought, the case went nowhere.

The pointy-headed would be rapist had an IQ of about six. He was barely able to blink without deep thought. He was found to be so mentally deficient he was unable to understand the consequences of his actions. Case closed. He would be free to rape again. And he would. We had some more run-ins with him in the following years until he was finally put where he would be among his peers: prison. What a wonderful system.

I worked with my friend a few more times after that arrest. He was great on domestics. He was a joy to work with and never came to work in a bad mood. He was very good at deescalating situations that could have led to violence. But, if shit went the wrong way, he could handle himself really well. My regular partner and I agreed to ask him to be the relief man on our car. He agreed. He was a great police officer.

Fast-forward about five years. We got a call of a person shot, an eleven-year-old girl. We interviewed the people at the scene. The victim's girlfriends told us she was talking to a boy outside her window. The boy brandished a handgun. She laughed at him and called him a fool. She told him the gun was not real. He pointed the gun at her, pulled the trigger, and shot her in the face. He blew her left eye out with the bullet exiting the rear of her head.

We wanted to get this fuck real bad. We did all the stuff we had to do at the scene, then went on the hunt. Initially, we got the stone-faced, arms-folded-across-the-chest gang bullshit. (The folded arms were one Chicago street gang's symbol of a five-pointed star. The points were the head, both shoulders, and both elbows.) They were "representing" their defiance of the police in front of the gathered crowd at the scene.

I swallowed my anger. Normally we did not let that shit slide, but we were trying to find out who the shooter was, so we made a temporary exception. My friend, who was a master at weaseling info from the factually challenged, got the name and address of the shooter. Even these thugs had some sense of moral justice when it involved an eleven-year-old. For whatever reason, one of them gave it up. Perhaps the shooter was not a member of their gang. We relocated to the shooter's home.

Again, my partner in speaking to the shooter's mother was able convince her that her son had to turn himself in. I often accused my friend of having an unholy, unwholesome relationship with the Blarney Stone of the "Old Sod." With the help of a couple other coppers, we were able to grab this guy up. He was a fifteen-year-old wannabe tough guy. He told us he never meant to shoot her. He told us he was sorry. Sorry as he may have been, he would be a lot sorrier very soon. For a good part of his young life, he would be hearing steel doors slam shut behind him. Still, he was alive. The young girl he had shot would laugh no more. He might one day have a chance at freedom. She would only know the freedom that death brings.

Not long after that arrest, my friend was hurt during a tussle with someone resisting arrest. He hurt his shoulder. For a while he was on light duty. My friend was a lot of fun. We had a great many good times "smokin' and jokin'." We had bounced down the avenues in a raggedy-assed police squadrol locking up the bad guys and hauling the dead.

Eventually, when the doctors could not fix his shoulder he was put on disability. He and his wife moved to the South where they lived on a ranch. I made it a habit to call him every Saint Patty's Day and every Christmas. When on Christmas I could not reach him I figured he was having phone problems out there in the boonies. In January, I found he was gone. He was a lovely man. He was kind. He was funny. A good soul. He was my friend. God Bless you Mikey. Rest in peace, brother.

<u>MICHAEL FRANCIS KINNALLY</u>
<u>END OF WATCH—JANUARY 1, 2012</u>

YOU GOT YOURS, I GOT...

We got a call of a "burglary in progress" at the store. We were told the guy was still in there. He got in through the back door. The alarm was triggered. We got there quick. He did not have time to escape. It was a Record/CD store. We searched the whole place. We found no one. We had the "zone" give us a mobile (radio to radio) with the desk. We asked them to go through the notification cards which were supposed to be filed by street, then by address.

If the beat officers on days or afternoons noticed a new business open, it behooved them to get a card for that business filled out. That would let us know whom to notify in case of fire or burglary. Otherwise, we had to sit on the place until the owner showed up to prevent possible crimes of opportunity. Imagine that.

Sometimes that took eight hours or more sitting on a store with a broken window or door. Watching some store owner's canned goods as cars flew by on the way to in-progress jobs was no way to spend an eight-hour tour.

The desk got in touch with the owner. He was on his way, but he was coming from a distance. That he was on the way was good news. My assist car and I still believed the burglar was somewhere in that store. The only place he could possibly be was in the ceiling. There was a ladder near the back door. He could have used it to get up in the ceiling. I got on the ladder with the other patrol officer steadying it so I could stand on the top. I looked into the ceiling. It was clear. But I did see an air conditioning/heating duct that went into the next store. That would be the only out for the bad guy.

I called the station again. I asked them to notify the owner of the other store. It turned out that it was the same guy who owned the first store. The second store appeared to be vacant and looked like it was being fixed up to rent. The owner of the stores got there pretty quickly. After he opened the door to the vacant store, we went through the whole place. Nothing. The owner had a ladder in that store as well, so I figured it was worth a shot to have a look up in the ceiling. While the other officer held the ladder again, I got up on the top step. I looked at the ceiling rafters.

At first I saw nothing, but something seemed out of place. It was a hump. The hump was the buttocks of the "Bubble-Butt Burglar." His girlfriend may have thought they were cute. Maybe his new state prison man friends would concur. It was kind of fitting, though, that his end resulted in his end, career wise. The Bubble-Butt Burglar was lying between the rafters. He had crawled from the other store using the space between the ductwork. I called out to him. He stuck his head up. After complying with orders given for our safety, he climbed down the ladder and was placed under arrest.

The owner of both businesses was very appreciative. He thanked us. We had him sign complaints on Bubble Butt. I was kind of surprised the owner of the businesses was black. True, we were in an all-black neighborhood, but the name on the store sounded like a German name. I asked why he had named the store Minz Music Store. He said, "No, no, it's like you got yours, and I got 'Minz.' This store is 'Minz.'" Case closed.

PAYLESS FOR PAYLESS SHOES

Payless Shoes, God Bless them. They tried to give it a go in the hood. Like so many other corporate businesses who felt it a civic duty to provide a decent-low priced product to a neighborhood that needed it, they tried and failed. They tried to provide jobs to a neighborhood that needed them. They tried and failed.

Here is an undeniable fact. Almost every attempt to open a major chain store in the 'hood has failed for only one reason. Crime. Kentucky Fried Chicken stores in the 'hood all without exception were the victims of armed robbery, gang activity, burglary, and looting. Same with McDonald's. Walgreens had an armed security guard. And so it goes. I am not sure how many stores are still there. If they are still there, I cannot see how they make any money at all. Maybe they feel as Payless did that it is their civic duty to remain.

In a city lot that was the former site of a neighborhood drug store, several storefronts were built. Baskin-Robbins put in a store. It was gone in a very short time. Dunkin' Donuts. There. Gone. A pizza place gave it a try. No deal. Gone. Payless stuck it out, however.

One night we got a call of a burglary in progress. It was about 2 a.m. A neighbor saw this guy chopping a hole in a flat-roofed building He was using a hatchet. Guess what store? If you guessed Payless Shoes, you are ready for your Inspector Clouseau decoder ring. Step up. This type of activity was kind of a common practice of the roof top burglars. They would chop a hole in the roof with a hatchet or axe until the hole was big enough to squeeze through. They would then drop in for a little thieving then break out with the loot. Sometimes the burglars broke their legs when dropping to the floor. Great spectator fun for the police. Their cries for help while we tried to gain entry to arrest them caused spontaneous laughter from the minions of the law.

On this particular thoroughfare, we had had a spate of burglaries with the same modus operandi. That guy was caught. This guy was probably an acolyte of the aforementioned burglar. Or, maybe it was just him returning to his previous occupation. Maybe he was an early release from prison for this nonviolent crime. That would really throw a wrench in our plan, which was the mass incarceration of people found guilty of nonviolent crimes.

Usually these criminals commit these non-violent crimes to get money to buy drugs. Drug use is also a non-violent crime that leads to more non-violent crime like burglary. Unlike violent crimes, unfortunately the victims of these non-violent crimes like burglary, auto theft, theft and shoplifting don't get a say in the early release of these non-violent criminals. Fuck em. The victims are just ordinary taxpaying shlubs. Why should they "matter?"

We had the desk notify the manager of the Payless store He came down and opened the steel security shutters to the store. Those steel shutters could probably withstand a nuclear blast. Too bad they had not installed a steel roof. We went in and searched the store, No luck. The burglar was gone. He was gone with about twenty-five pairs of woman's shoes. He left the boxes in disarray on the floor. We surmised that he must have had a plastic garbage bag to carry the loot. He had probably escaped through the self-locking steel back door which was no impediment to breaking out of the business.

At the time, we had an evidence tech assigned to our district. Besides being a crackerjack evidence tech, he was a great copper. He arrived at the scene and looked the place over. He went behind the store to see how the guy got up to the roof. He went up the stairs of an adjacent building to see what our caller had seen. On the way, down he checked the basement stairwell of that building. Guess who he found with a garbage bag full of lady's shoes? He found a non-violent criminal burglar. How discriminatory. Shame on that competent police officer.

We had gotten there so fast that the non-violent burglar had to hide in a basement stairwell lest we see him with his large bag of shoes. I mean, at 2 am, how many people would be walking down the alley with a large plastic garbage bag of lady's shoes. We had a patrol car not far from where he was hiding. They were watching the back of the store. With those officers still posted there, it would have been unsafe for the non-violent criminal to carry off his loot.

So, bottom line, another nonviolent criminal would be off to a state-supported job making license plates or whatever they do now to keep the nonviolent criminals busy. Maybe they have a prison shoemaker shop. Our nonviolent criminal could plan to burglarize that. He had wanted to pay less for Payless shoes. Thanks to a pack of law dogs, he would drink the bitter vinegar of defeat. Payless eventually pulled out. It had tried and failed. PS Our plan of mass incarceration was working!

CFD PARAMEDICS

The CFD paramedics were great. Ambulances CFD-15 and CFD-23 were the ones we saw most frequently. They were with us on many of the calls we responded to, in which our victims or sometimes offenders had to be treated for injuries. They tried to treat everyone the same, even if they were the attackers involved in a violent incident.

Oftentimes, they had to treat a steady stream of wounded bad guys, sometimes while their patient was handcuffed. Sometimes the paramedics also had a police officer jammed in the back with them while they transported offenders or victims to a hospital. It was our preference to transport the bad guys in a wagon if they were not hurt too badly, but sometimes because of injuries, that was not possible.

Many times, the paramedics had to work on and transport very violent or mentally challenged people. It was no "hot stone" massage after a dip in a Jacuzzi. Sometimes, they had to put spit masks on the real crazies to keep from being spit upon. They also had to tape some of these guys to the board they used to carry them, not only to prevent them from injuring themselves further but also to prevent the violent crazies from injuring them. Like us, the paramedics wanted to go home uninjured and alive. For the most part, it was a totally thankless job.

The paramedics always responded to our scenes of mayhem quickly. Sometimes they got there before us, depending on how busy we were. That was very dangerous for them. Many times, the bad guys did not want the other bad guys to survive their efforts to kill them. That put the paramedics in the bull's-eye. The paramedics were not armed, so it was pretty courageous of them to arrive at a chaotically violent scene without the police there to mitigate that chaos. They went anyway. They never slowed down.

They also took care of us when we got a booboo. They gave us aspirins, slapped a bandage on our owies, wiped our tears, then sent us back to the checkerboard of daily of violence. Normally, they were so overburdened with calls that the Chicago Fire Department had to start sending ladder trucks and pumpers to the scenes of gang and drug violence.

The ambulances assigned to Chicago Police "working districts" rolled all day and all night. The only time I saw them stop was when they stopped at a hospital or fire house to load up on supplies they needed. That says a lot about the culture of the Chicago Fire Department. It also says a lot about the character of their version of our street grunts.

Thank you, Chicago Fire Department paramedics, for all you did and continue to do.

ANOTHER LOVELY MAN

When I finally got through with my mandatory period of training with my FTO, I was assigned to a one-man car on the day watch. That is when I realized that after all the training in the academy and with my FTOs, I didn't know anything about being a patrolman. It would take years and many missteps to measure up to most of the guys I initially worked with.

The first time I was working alone, I couldn't remember anything concerning reports or notifications. All the things I thought I would do, if given my freedom to do so, I realized were unrealistic or undoable. I was at square zero. My first job was to take a report on a stolen auto. All of a sudden, I could remember nothing about which report to use or who to notify. Just when I was starting to freak out, a patrol car pulled up. It was a two-man car. These guys had been partners for a while, and they had heard me get the call. They had about four or five years on at the time. In my little corner of the world, that made them vets. They helped me avoid the pitfalls of improper reporting. These guys did not have to help me, but they did.

You learned really fast by necessity in high-crime areas. You got more calls for service and did more street stops. You made more arrests and had more court cases. At the end of the day, you became more proficient by necessity. At the end of each watch, all your reports were turned in to a checkoff supervisor to be approved or redone. The bottom line was that you wanted to do them right.

On many of the jobs I was assigned when I was new, those vets just showed up although they were not assigned. Perhaps someone had helped them when they were the new kid on the block. Maybe they were paying it back. Whatever the reason I was glad for their help.

About three years later, I was on a violent domestic disturbance. Boyfriend had taken Girlfriend's gold chain to the dope man in exchange for drugs. There was screaming plus threats aplenty. Before we got there, some pushing and shoving had occurred, and we got that boil down to a simmer.

Boyfriend was told he would have to leave. He was unhappy. During his unhappiness, he was pumping up his man cred' by shouting epithets at the police. That made us unhappy. As he was getting his jacket, he shoved yours truly from his path. Now Boyfriend was going to be much unhappier. He and I both started to throw hands in a narrow hallway. All of a sudden, I saw a hand appear near Boyfriend's neck. Boyfriend fell to the ground unconscious. It seemed to me some sort of police voodoo black magic had laid him low. One second he was throwing a left. The next second he was on the floor.

It was my friend. He had used a law-dog version of the Vulcan nerve pinch. Boyfriend was cuffed and led away. He was in a state of bafflement. So was I. My friend just smiled.

He and his partner transferred from the district years later when a watch commander requested they join him in a different district. They were great guys. Eventually, his partner was promoted to the rank of sergeant, following in his father's footsteps. The new sergeant's partner was David Graney. Dave was a lovely man with a beautiful smile and a hearty laugh. He was a hell of a card player and a workin' police. He died while standing at the front desk of his new district while answering a phone. He had a heart attack.

Thanks for your help Dave. I hope the angels know not to get in a game of seven card stud with you. Rest easy brother. God Bless.

JESUS IS IN THE JOINT

I was working days. I got a call of a woman stabbed in the house. I activated my emergency equipment then headed to the address given. When I arrived a fire department pumper was at the scene. They were preparing to leave. One of the firemen was carrying one of their larger fire extinguishers. I rushed up the stairs to the front door of the home. I was met at the door by the woman who had been slashed with a knife. She had her hand wrapped in a makeshift bandage. The hallway I was standing in had been on fire a few minutes ago.

I asked for a description of the offender. She gave me one and I sent it out. I told her I would be back to do the report after I first saw if I could pick up the offender. I got in my car and hit the alley behind the house. About a half block down, I saw my guy carrying a gas can. I grabbed him up, secured the gas can in the passenger area of the squad car, and returned to the scene, where the complainant identified "Mr. BurnUout." He was trucked off to the district for processing. An evidence tech processed the gas can at the scene, as those volatile and flammable liquids were not sent through the normal evidentiary channels.

The backstory to the commotion is this. The whole family was playing cards. Everybody was winning except Mr. BurnUout. Mr. BurnUout's mama was laughing at him. Mr. BurnUout's sisters and brother were laughing at him. He accused them of cheating him. He was a poor loser. He stood up and went into his mother's bedroom. Mom was a sickly woman. Mr. BurnUout had bought Mom a compact refrigerator for her medications. He took it off its stand, ripping the electric cord from the outlet.

He was headed out the door with the refrigerator when Sis confronted him. A struggle ensued during which Mr. BurnUout pulled his pocketknife on Sis. She laughed at him while calling him a fool. He advanced on her, and she grabbed the knife. He pulled it from her, cutting her hand. It was a deep cut. She wrapped it in a dish towel. He left the refrigerator and fled, not to escape but to exact revenge on those who laughed at him.

Mr. BurnUout went to the garage and retrieved an empty gas can. He walked to a nearby service station, bought a gallon of gasoline, came back to the house, splashed gasoline in the hallway, then set it afire. He would have the last laugh. He would burn the house down. The quick response by fire and police stopped that scenario from happening.

Mr. BurnUout committed an aggravated battery and an aggravated arson. Both were felonies. But then, the Cook County rule of the offender being a family member kicked in. The state attorney did not believe the family members would testify. If the family did not testify, the state attorney would lose the case. Their stats would suffer. That would be unacceptable. In their defense, I must say, if they charged everyone who deserved it with a felony, the cases would be backed up five to seven years in the courts. The charges were knocked down to simple battery and damage to property. Those charges were misdemeanors. The family did show up in a lower court, and Mr. BurnUout was convicted of the misdemeanors. The judge gave him jail time with a proviso that he receive, a mental evaluation and treatment while in jail.

I ran into him about a year later. He apologized for how he had acted while in custody. Then he said what I had heard over a hundred times in my career. He had found Jesus in the Cook County jail. I guess a lot of cons can identify with Jesus. Jesus the man was arrested, judged and put to death. I guess His word will touch some people in deep despair. Where else would Jesus be, if his purpose was to save the damned? I can think of no other place where Jesus could do more good. He certainly would not be at a $12,000-a-plate dinner for a political candidate. The people in prison are at least savable.

TOO SLOW

I was working with a new officer. I think her FTO was taking a sick day, so the new officer was placed with me. We went on a few routine calls on which no police action was required. Then we got a call to go to a hospital regarding a possible child abuse.

Doctors were required to call police in any case in which they thought abuse might be involved. There were certain injuries that could happen that may look like child abuse but could also be a normal active-kid injury. The doctors in most cases could tell the difference. Elbow, knee, and broken-bone injuries on smaller children were the most common. Usually that came with some bruising near the injured area. These injuries were usually caused by twisting or pulling a child's arm or leg.

Sometimes children were scalded because they had either defecated or urinated in their clothing or bed. They were put in water that was scalding hot to teach them a lesson. There was also shaken-baby syndrome in which a parent shook an infant to make it stop crying or any other behavior that they thought was irritating. This sometimes led to brain damage or death.

There were injuries to rectums, penises, and vaginas, usually due again to the child's bathroom habits. There was also sudden infant death syndrome (SIDS). This usually happened from leaving an infant face down in soft bedding. In some cases, SIDS occurred when the parents and baby slept in the same bed. One or the other of the parents would roll over on the infant and unknowingly smother it. That was not the medical cause of death but what the doctors attributed it to in some cases. There was also malnourishment or lack of care, such as not getting inoculations against childhood ailments.

It was usually doctors or nurses who first noticed the many signs of abuse or neglect when a child was brought to the hospital emergency room for treatment. We sometimes got in the mix when, while on a call, we observed filthy, unsanitary conditions or lack of food in the home. Depending on the circumstances, in those cases, we acted to arrest for neglect or take the child from the home. We also called DCFS (Department of Children and Family Services) to check on conditions in some homes we visited where conditions were borderline.

That said, when we arrived at the hospital, we inquired who called and why. A nurse took us in the back. Our victim was in one of the curtained-off areas. He was eight years old and had a bandage over his eye. I asked the doctor to lift the bandage to show me the injury, although we also would also get the technical jargon from his report. The child otherwise looked to be in good physical shape and was properly dressed. The injury was an area of swelling around the eye with some damage to the blood vessels. The vessels in the eye were broken and some bleeding had occurred causing a bloody spot in the white of the eye. There was also another mark under the eye; I guess you could call it a laceration.

I asked the kid what happened. He told me his mother hit him with a belt. The problem was that she hit him with the buckle end of the belt. He was very lucky he did not lose the eye. I asked why she hit him. He said it was because he was running late while getting ready for school. I went to interview the mother who was standing nearby. She wondered why the police were involved. I asked why she had hit her son with a belt. She replied that she had to get him off to school, then go to work. She said he was moving too slow.

The mother was a nicely dressed woman in business attire. She was holding an infant. Her male friend was standing nearby. I told her to give the infant to the female police officer. I told her that she was under arrest. She seemed shocked. She asked "Why? I told her the arrest was for hitting her son in the eye with a belt buckle. She claimed that hitting him in the face was an accident. She had meant to hit him across the back. Hadn't she had brought him to the hospital to be treated? Yes, but if she did not, his school teacher would probably have alerted the police.

In many cases of this sort, we saw certain similarities. Many of the people accused of child abuse had themselves been punished in the same way. They saw nothing wrong with it. After all, had they not grown up to be normal? In the end, hitting a child in the face with a belt because he was moving too slow is unacceptable.

Child abuse knows no gender, race, or class distinctions. In this case, arrest was called for because of the severity of the injury. Boyfriend then unwisely tried to interject himself into the mix. But, after some frank counseling, he withdrew from the arrest process. We took the mother in and referred the case to DCFS. Will that kid grow up without long-lasting problems? Maybe. Maybe not. I will leave you with this thought: You can tell the best of us by how we treat the least of us.

NEEDLEWORK

U sually when we had cause to stop someone, it was based on the information we received from a caller. Otherwise, we did street stops when we had a reasonable suspicion that somebody had committed a crime, was committing a crime, or was about to commit a crime. When we did a stop, it usually involved searches for weapons or other instruments related to the commission of a crime. A satchel full of tools or a simple screwdriver or hammer, when carried down the alley during the day, could be used to commit a burglary. Narcotics could be carried anywhere, including the mouth and hair.

Some auto thieves carried a Slim Jim down their pant leg. The Slim Jim is a thin metal strip two to three feet in length that is shoved down in the space between the outside of a car window and the rubber gasket on the car door. By working the Slim Jim up and down, the car's door lock can be compromised and the door opened. An innocent-looking screwdriver can be used to crack the steering column on older cars to compromise the ignition system and start the car.

There is also a piece of plastic that looks like a guitar pick that is called a *jiggler*, which could be inserted into an ignition switch to steal a certain make of foreign cars. Other jigglers are key-shaped metal pieces that compromise door locks and ignition switches. We found key rings that had keys that were filed down to shove in an ignition key slot so if a police officer looked at an ignition switch, it looked like the driver had the keys to the vehicle.

So, to prevent crime, street stops plus information gathering are a necessary part of the job. Most stops are not pleasant; they are all dangerous. Other than weapons, one of the most dangerous implements of crime we faced were hypodermic needles. At the time, possession of a hypodermic needle without a doctor's prescription was a crime. The first question we asked before a search was conducted was, "Do you have anything on you that is going to hurt me like a knife, a razor, or needles? Anything sharp?" The usual replies were, "Yes, I have one or the other" or "No, I do not." However, because we mostly dealt with criminals and the drug addled, sometimes they lied or forgot.

A friend of mine told me while training a new recruit that he had conducted a street stop in a high-drug-traffic area. He asked the usual questions during the interrogation and search. Then, as the new recruit conducted a pat-down search for weapons and drugs, he got stuck by a hypodermic needle.

This was potentially a life-changing or life-ending development for the new guy. AIDS and hepatitis C are both diseases that at some point can become fatal. Intravenous drug users helped to spread these diseases because of needle sharing. Usually, some blood from the person who injected the controlled substance remains in the barrel of the syringe and the hollow needle. If the hypodermic needle is used again, that blood will be mixed with the next batch of whatever substance that person injects. So, getting stuck was not a good thing.

As soon as the recruit got stuck, the dope fiend took off running. He was immediately pursued, his adrenaline kicked in. He disappeared into one of the many hiding places available to a fleeing criminal in the 'hood. The police officers involved in the stop made it their business to look for the shitbird nightly. Their persistence paid off when he was apprehended near the same spot about a week later. Since the criminal had compromised an officer's health by failing to reveal the hypodermic needle on his person, he was deemed untrustworthy. His search this time would be conducted in a private setting where he could not conceal any dangerous objects that could harm another police officer. He was transported to the district station. Before he hit the lockup to jeopardize anyone else's health, he was escorted into the back of an unmanned police squadrol. The senior training officer volunteered to do the search.

Many of the hypes do not want to give up their "works," which usually consist of a hypodermic syringe, a spoon, a deep metal bottle cap for mixing water with a powdered drug, a candle, or lighter. This is necessary for heating and dissolving the mix contained in the spoon into an injectable liquid. Add to these items some cotton balls, which are used to filter the liquid as it is siphoned into the syringe. A cloth or leather case completes the basic kit.

As most addicts are accustomed to their particular works, they are inclined to resist their confiscation by police. In this case during the search, the arrestee resisted the officer's confiscation of his drug paraphernalia. During the struggle, the violent offender managed to stab himself numerous times with his favorite syringe. How stupid of him to resist the confiscation. Now the needle on his favorite syringe was bent so it could never be used again. How sad for "Mr. Addict." He was not a nice man.

Mr. Addict would have time to reflect on his stupidity in our think tank. He just could not see how our efforts were meant to help him withdraw from his terrible habit. Mr. Addict was brought to the redemptive process. It was the best we could do for the poor, unfortunate soul. Fortunately, the officer who was stuck with the needle lived to retire from the job without evident health problems.

Thank you, guardian angel of new coppers, for helping your earthbound brothers once again defeat the forces of evil.

BLACK COPS, WHITE COPS, HISPANIC COPS, ASIAN COPS

The bad guys do not care what color or ethnic group police belong to. Neither should you.

When we pull up in our blue and white to stop criminal activity, the bad guys are not looking at our color. They will try to defeat our efforts to arrest them because we are wearing the blue or any of the other colors street grunts wear throughout the free world.

Look at the list of officers killed in the line of duty in Chicago. They are representative of all of us. We are you.

If you happened to be in an overturned car that is on fire, would you care what color the men who came to save you were? I think not. We don't care what gender, color, religion, or ethnicity you are either; we will pull you out of that metaphorical burning car because it's what we do.

BURGLARS

Burglary is the kind of sneaky crime everybody hates. No one wants to come home to find their home or apartment torn apart. If it is not bad enough that someone was rooting through your possessions, you then you discover that some of your possessions have been removed. You feel kind of violated. You feel angry.

Commercial burglaries are bad, but home burglaries are more personal. Home burglaries usually take place during the day. The burglar takes away your sense of safety. If the burglar has been watching your home, he knows you are not there. If he is just some junkie, he may not care if you are home or not. That is when shit can go way wrong. A break-in while you are home then becomes a home invasion/robbery. This is a much more serious offense. Most burglars know this and will retreat if there is someone in the house. It could also be dangerous for the burglar if the homeowner is armed. His career in burglary might come to a sudden end.

Most burglaries go unnoticed until the homeowner arrives home and discovers the crime. At that point, all we can do is take a report to document time, method of entry and exit, and items taken. From this information, we can develop patterns and methods of operation. Some burglaries, however, are called in by a nosey neighbor who notices something or someone that looks wrong. Some are stopped or solved by alert police officers doing their jobs. Here are a few in which the law dogs won.

UNREQUITED LOVE AND THE TRICKY WEASEL

I was working a one-man car on days when a burglary-in-progress call was broadcast. Multiple units responded. It was a large apartment building with maybe thirty apartments. Some cars went to the back; others pulled up in front. Of course, the burglary was on the third floor. We found the apartment. It looked like the entry/exit was the rear porch window and door.

We searched the apartment for the offender as he could be hiding in a closet or under a bed. It was not readily apparent what was missing. The TV was still in its spot, but all the drawers in the bedroom dressers were pulled out. The contents of the drawers were strewn on the floor. The thief was probably looking for cash and jewelry hidden in the drawers.

The assisting units were searching the upper stairways because sometimes if we got to the scene quickly enough, the burglar would go to the floors above the burglary, then walk down like he lives there. Tricky weasels, they are.

Basement stairways were also checked. In this particular case, the rear stairways on the apartment buildings were connected. So, despite our efforts, there were numerous other avenues of escape. If the bad guy had taken only money and jewelry, he could have walked right by us since those items are easily concealable.

We found the apartment resident's work number after calling numerous numbers in a phone book near the telephone. She said she still had to stay at work for a while but would come home as soon as possible. We notified the building manager about the jimmied porch window. We asked him to secure the apartment. We told our victim to call when she got home to make a report when she determined what was missing. Most of the cars that had responded had already left. A couple of us were still in front of the building, when to our great surprise, out of the alley walked "Mr. Tricky Weasel" with a black plastic garbage bag slung over his shoulder. Hmm.

Mr. Tricky Weasel did a kind of "oh, fuck" stutter step. The black plastic garbage bag was derisively called "ghetto luggage" by the 'hood rats. Sometimes burglars would put the proceeds of their burglaries in the black plastic garbage bags, then conceal them in trash receptacles in the alley. They would come back later for the loot when the police had left the scene. Those weasels they were tricky.

Mr. Tricky Weasel walked right into our weasel trap. We stopped him, of course. We asked to look in his bag. We found many items that looked like they could have been taken from our victim's apartment. He also had a really good story. He told us that the victim was his girlfriend. He said that they had broken up, and he had been asked to get his things out of the apartment. He had even taken a framed picture of his one true love, our victim, and placed it in his bag.

Mr. Weasel said he had forgotten his key then used the window to get in. It was a sad and beautiful story of a precious love gone awry. We wiped our tears. We asked his true love's name. Alas, although it had been emblazoned on his scarred heart only minutes ago, he had already put her in his rear-view mirror. He had forgotten the name of his one true love.

We shackled Mr. Tricky Weasel to detain him while we continued our investigation. A quick phone call to the victim confirmed that his fantasy love affair was just that. We told her to meet us at the station where Mr. Tricky Weasel was about to be processed then sent to a place where he could make new romantic friends.

Tricky Weasel Trappers - 1 – Tricky Weasel - 0.
Case closed.

THE NOSEY NEIGHBOR VS. THE BACKDOOR BURGLAR

I saw from reports that a burglary had been committed in my area of responsibility. I went to check out the address. I knew it was an apartment building. The point of entry was a rear door. Miracle of miracles, it was on the first floor. I went to the rear porch to check it out.

While I was on the rear porch the woman who lived in the house next door opened her window and gave me a shout. I left the porch and went to talk to her. I had spoken to her before. She was a great source of neighborhood goings on. She came to all the C.A.P.S. (Chicago Alternative Policing Strategy) beat meetings. She was elderly and lived alone. She had a voice that probably could be heard by low flying aircraft.

She asked if I was investigating the burglary. I answered in the affirmative. She told me she had seen the burglar. I asked her what had happened. She told me at first, she did not know it was a burglary. But she said she "smelled a rat" when she saw the burglar walk out of the victim's rear door with a TV. I asked why she did not call 911. She told me that he had a red truck parked in the alley. On the side of the truck, written in large, white letters, was "Moe's Appliance Repair." The man put the TV in the truck and drove off. She wondered why he had left the door of the apartment open. It stayed open until the apartment resident came home and found his TV missing.

The woman said she waited until she saw me because she knew I would do something. I thanked her for the info. She told me, "Wait a minute; I have more." She went into her kitchen and came back with a piece of paper, on which was written the license-plate number of the truck. She had used binoculars to see it from her bedroom window. I could have kissed her. I did a supplementary report to the burglary with the info. I ran the plate and came up with a name. I ran the name for a rap sheet and photo. I did a photo array for my nosey-neighbor crime fighter. She picked him out.

I called my contacts in suburban departments that bordered my beat. Two days later, a suburban copper caught the Backdoor Burglar in the act. He ran. They brought him down, and he was arrested. He had been hitting their suburb pretty good. They tied him to numerous burglaries. He was on parole for…burglary. Bye-bye, Backdoor Burglar!

The suburban department gave me an "attaboy." I went by my nosey-neighbor crime fighter's home and thanked her. I said we got him because of your sharp eyes. She blushed.

Nosey-Neighbor Crime Fighter - 1 - Backdoor Burglar – 0
Case closed.

THE SHARP-EYED OFFICER VS. THE B. S. CARPENTER

I got a call from another officer, who asked for a meet. I was not working my beat that day, but met the officer on what was normally my beat. She was a good cop. She told me that she had spotted a guy in a doorway with a lot of carpentry tools. They were almost all high-end power tools. We both went to question this guy.

He was about eighteen years old and told us that he was a carpenter. He said some guy did not pay him for a job he had done, and he was forced to sell his tools for some cash. We were very sad about his financial dilemma. I asked where he planned to sell them, and he told me he was going to the secondhand store a half block down. We asked why he was in this doorway around the corner and a half block from the store? He said the store was not open, and he did not want to stand out there with all these high-end tools.

I asked for some ID. He lived in a suburb a few miles from our city limits. I asked why he came all this way to our fair city and how he managed to get here. All his answers seemed dishonest and unsatisfactory based on what we observed. To top it off, he said his van had broken down and the police had driven him here. That part was true.

I asked to see his hands. They were as soft as a baby's butt. If he was a carpenter, I was Winnie the Pooh. We took him in for investigation. Unbeknown to him, he had inadvertently camped in a doorway, fifteen feet from two of my very own resident burglars. If they had not been in their drug-induced naps, this guy would have had nothing left but a few lumps on his bean. So, we were actually doing him a favor. Otherwise, how could he call the police and tell the law dogs that someone had stolen his stolen stuff?

Our specious carpenter kept asking if he was under arrest. I told him that he was detained for investigation regarding his so-called property as he had no receipts for same. Sadly, if I could not find an owner, although I could keep the property, I could only hit him with a minor charge instead of a burglary. If he was legit, he could come back with some proof of ownership to re-claim the property.

I got on the phone to the suburban police department where he said he lived. Guess what? They knew him. What luck. I asked for their detectives. When I got a dick on the line, I asked him to check his reports for power tools taken in a burglary. Bingo. That very morning, the property in possession of "Mr. B. S. Carpenter" was taken in a garage burglary. I happily informed Mr. B.S. Carpenter he was under arrest. The back story to this felonious saga is as follows.

Mr. B. S. Carpenter broke into a neighbor's garage. He had seen the tools on occasion as his neighbor worked in his garage. He kicked in the side door, loaded the tools into his piece-of-crap van, and then drove it until it broke down. Mr. B. S. Carpenter had driven toward our fair city so his local police could not find the stolen merchandise in any of the local pawn shops or secondhand stores. He had outsmarted his dumb self. He unloaded the tools onto a street corner in an adjoining suburb. The new plan was to take the bus with his loot. One of our patrol cars spotted him, and the officers bought his story; they thought he was legit. They offered to take him to where he told them he had a job. He was dropped off where we found him.

If that female officer had not spotted him, he probably would have fenced the stolen power tools and been on his way with a pocketful of cash. But thanks to a sharp-eyed police officer, his plan to enrich himself at his neighbor's expense was foiled. When the suburban coppers wrote him up, he would be going to county to await trial for his un-neighborly deed. That sharp-eyed officer eventually made sergeant. Unfortunately, about five years later, cancer took her life. Rest in peace, sister. Good job.

Sharp-Eyed Officer – 1 - Mr. B. S. Carpenter - 0.
Case closed.

THE CYNICAL MEN IN BLUE VS. MR. JOCKEY SHORTS

I was working the day watch when a call of a burglary in progress came out. The info we had was that a man had entered through the front window of a garden apartment. It was a three-story building. We got there fairly quickly, and another police car pulled up in back as we pulled up in front. If the burglar was still in there, we had him contained.

We looked in the window of the garden apartment. We saw a young man in his underwear. Well, since he was in his underwear many might say he probably lived there. Not so, was what the law dogs of Fort Forgotten would say. We had seen this sort of behavior before.

Many times, a burglar who knew the home's occupants were at work would stay in the house or apartment most of the day. He would use the bathroom, watch TV, make something to eat, and rummage through the place at his leisure. Many times, this type of burglar would relieve themselves in places other than the toilet. Why? I do not know but do it they did. Sometimes, the dummies even fell asleep on the couch only to awoken by an angry resident or the police. Their thought process is a mystery.

We let the other units responding know we had someone in the apartment. We entered the building and knocked on the door. "Mr. Jockey Shorts" answered the door. We inquired about his presence in the apartment. He said it was his auntie's apartment. He said he had been suspended from school and had called her because his parents were at work. His auntie lived near the school and told him he could stay there until his parents came home. She told him she had left a window unlocked because she had once forgotten her key. It was quite a yarn the young Mr. Jockey Shorts was spinning for the cynical men in blue.

We asked for his auntie's name and phone number to confirm his story. He gave us a name but said she could not be reached at work. He said she worked on the factory floor with no way to receive a call. Mr. Jockey Shorts was quite the accomplished liar. He even had an unfinished bowl of cereal on the kitchen table.

Another copper going through the apartment found his pants with his ID in the pocket. He was twenty years old. Our metaphorical scissors had just cut his metaphorical yarn. He just smiled and turned around to be cuffed. We let him get dressed first while we searched the apartment for the resident's phone book.

We finally came up with a contact number. We confirmed our suspicions about Mr. Jockey Shorts. We told the apartment resident to meet us in the station, and off we went with the young Mr. Jockey Shorts.

I suggested that since he was such an accomplished liar that he seek political office. He said, "Hmm."

Cynical Men in Blue - 1 - Mr. Jockey Shorts – 0
Case closed.

A TALE OF TWO LAWN MOWERS

LAWN MOWER I

I got a call to meet an officer on another beat. He wanted a back-up to check somebody out. When I got there, the other officer pointed to the guy he wanted to stop. Mr. Lawnmower Man was a super-sized version of the average man. He was pushing a brand-new lawnmower down the alley. We approached him to inquire his purpose in pushing his lawnmower in the alley.

Most people did not walk their lawn mowers down the alley. Most lawn mowers were used, then put away in a garage. He said he was in the lawn-mowing business. Mr. Lawn Mower Man said that he was going door-to-door looking for work. We surmised that from the surreptitious route he had chosen in an alley, that he was trying to not be seen by any prospective lawn-mowing customers. Perhaps, though, he was trying to go unseen by the true owner of the lawn mower he possessed or the police.

I asked Mr. Lawn Mower Man to tell me, without looking, the brand name of his new mower. He failed my primitive lie-detector test. He just could not recall the brand of his new mower. Amid his loud protestations of "Why you fuckin' with me?" Mr. Lawn Mower Man was cuffed and detained for further investigation.

We took Mr. Lawn Mower Man into our investigatory hub. We had him and the lawn mower but nothing more. I volunteered to go back to where we found him and try to find the owner of the pilfered mower.

I started with the block where we found him. I went door-to-door on both sides of the street. No luck. I relocated to the previous block and started the process all over. There were some houses I could skip as they had no lawns. What they did have was garbage-strewn mud.

I got lucky on the second house on the block. This house had a nicely maintained green lawn. An older man answered the door.

He related he had that type of mower, but it was in the garage. We went to look. His garage door was unlocked, and his mower was gone. Mr. Lawn Mower Man was probably the culpable party. I asked the mower's owner if he had a receipt for his mower since it was still pretty new. He did, plus he had the serial number. It would be bye-bye time for Mr. Lawn Mower Man if the numbers matched.

I returned to the station with my victim and checked the mower. Bingo. The serial numbers matched. My co-worker in the meantime had run Mr. Lawn Mower Man for previous criminal activity. Bingo again. He was wanted on warrants for failure to appear, plus he was on parole for burglary. Mr. Lawn Mower Man could now be gainfully employed mowing the lawn outside the warden's office.

Some may ask why we went through so much work for what seemed to be such a minor crime. It certainly was not the Lufthansa heist or the Brinks armored truck robbery, but to this elderly gentleman, it would have been several hundred dollars out of his pocket. When you are on Social Security, several hundred dollars is a big deal.

This is what police do. We try to get some justice for the little guy. In this case, because of a sharp-eyed beat copper, we returned the elderly man's property to him, plus we took a bad guy off the street. The elderly man shook our hands and thanked us. That alone made our efforts worthwhile.

Hard-Working Coppers – 1 - Lawn Mower Man – 0
Case closed.

LAWN MOWER II

We were working a beat car on afternoons. It was winter. It had snowed in dribs and drabs most of the day. Some sidewalks were shoveled, most were not. We pulled up to the traffic light at a major intersection. As usual we were unconsciously scanning for the out of order while we conversed about the merits of thin crust versus deep dish pizzas. To our surprise, we saw a short bundled up man pushing a lawnmower.

We hung a left then cut a U-turn to come up behind him. He was next to a school where the walk had been shoveled. We got out of the car. We asked just what in the fuck he was doing pushing a lawn mower down the street in a snowstorm.

He knew we had eyeballed him, so he had a minute to think of a story. He said he was a lawn mower repairman, and he was returning the lawn mower to its owner. The usually stone-faced interrogators of wrongdoers laughed out loud at his spurious attempt to con the men in blue.

We said, "OK, let's go deliver this mower together." We put the mower in the trunk. After a search of his person, we put "Mr. Lawn Mower Repairman" in the back seat of our safe and secure city-owned limo. He directed us up the street about two blocks. We went down a side street. He told us where to stop.

He pointed to the house from whence he had been given the job of repairing the lawn mower. I knocked on the door, and a senior citizen answered the door. I asked if he had a lawn mower. He answered in the affirmative. I asked him to see his mower. I explained that our hardworking Mr. Lawn Mower Repairman had related to us that he had gotten a lawn mower from his property to repair.

We went to the basement, and his lawn mower was gone. I asked him to step outside to see if the lawn mower we had was his. He threw on a coat and out we went. By God, it was his mower. We asked if he had given permission to the owl-hoot in our back seat to repair or possess his lawn mower for any reason; he replied that he had not. We asked our victim to meet us at the station to sign complaints. We told him he could take possession of his property after we had inventoried it as evidence for the court case. He agreed.

We cuffed Mr. Lawn Mower Repairman after placing him formally under arrest. On the way to the station, we asked why he had taken us to the home of his burglary victim. He just shrugged. We made a couple suppositions.

Supposition One: He took the mower to the dope man. The boorish staff of the dope man impolitely told him to take his raggedy-ass, out-of-season lawn mower and remove himself from their venue of commerce. Rebuffed by the dope man's rude personnel, our guy was going to try to sell it on the boulevards of our fair city, where he was spotted by Johnny Law.

Supposition Two: Mr. Lawn Mower Repairman was cold, out of money, hungry, and with no friends or family whom he had not stolen from. Therefore, he may have wanted the security of the penal system. We, Johnny Laws, called persons of his ilk "Institutionalized Men." These were people who were more comfortable with the rules of the prison system than they were with the rules on the outside. It was familiar to them. You did not have to seek a job; you were given one. You did not have to grocery shop; it was done for you. You were told when to get up, when to sleep, and when to eat. You could work out in the prison yard and build your muscles to make yourself more attractive to the guys on your tier.

Mr. Lawn Mower Repairman was mum as to his reasoning for taking us to the home of his victim, mainly because he had fallen asleep in the back seat, thus once again proving *Officer Murphy's Maxim*: "If they sleep, they're guilty."

Johnny Laws – 1 - Lawn Mower Repairman – 0
Case closed.

FANTASY ISLAND
('HOOD STYLE)

I was working a one-man car on the day watch. I was assigned to a call of a woman screaming for help. Several cars volunteered to back me up. We all hit the address at about the same time. It was a three-story building, and the problem was on the third floor (Who would've thunk it?). Two of us went up the front stairs while the other car covered the rear.

When we got to the third floor, we found the front door kicked in. We cautiously entered the apartment with our weapons drawn while calling out our office. We heard sobbing coming from the rear of the apartment. In the kitchen, we found a woman who had been beaten and choked. There were visible injuries to her face and bruising to her neck. A further investigation revealed that her boyfriend, "Mr. Door Kicker," had done the damage to the door and to "Ms. Sob Lady."

As in so many cases of love gone wrong, the altercation was about real or perceived infidelity. We looked for Mr. Door Kicker but came up negative. I wrote a battery case report and included the damage to the door. I advised Ms. Sob Lady how to get a warrant for Mr. Door Kicker's arrest. I also explained how to get an order of protection. Both options required her to go before a judge. I left after helping to secure her door until she could have it properly fixed.

I was gone less than forty minutes when a call of woman screaming for help at the same address was dispatched. I told the zone I would take it. A few cars volunteered to back me up. I trundled up the stairway again. After I left, Mr. Door Kicker had returned, kicked in the door, and then battered his one true love once again. I did another report and advised the woman to stay with family or friends until we took Mr. Door Kicker into custody.

Ms. Sob Lady was a CTA bus driver. She lived only a block from the route she drove. The next day, Mr. Door Kicker attacked Ms. Sob Lady on the street as she waited for a bus to start her shift as a driver. This time, he also took her CTA driver's badge after battering her. Again, another case report was written, this time for a strong-arm robbery. This guy was really starting to piss me off. So now, my daily self-assigned task was to apprehend Mr. Door Kicker. I told the victim to call immediately if she saw him.

As best I could, I tried to stay near her location. I was camped out in an alley near Ms. Sob Lady's third-floor apartment. I was rewarded for my vigilance when the call came out again. I hustled over to the building and pulled up in the rear, as that had been Mr. Door Kicker's method of flight in the previous incidents. I saw Mr. Door Kicker coming down the rear stairway about the same time he saw me. He ran back up the stairs to Ms. Sob Lady's apartment.

I climbed those stairs for what I hoped to be the last time. I got on the radio and told my assist cars that he might be coming out the front. I grabbed him just as he reached the damaged front door. After a brief tussle, the door-kicking love beast was cuffed. Mr. Door Kicker was subsequently headed for a place where he would damage his door-kicking foot on our steel-doored accommodations.

Complaints were signed. Supplementary reports to the different cases were completed. A Cook County state attorney refused the felony robbery charges; the robbery was downgraded to a theft and a battery. Mr. Door Kicker was charged, and Ms. Sob Lady was given a court date. On the court date, I was sitting in the front of the courtroom with my fellow officers waiting for our cases to be called. We all were rubbernecking trying to find our victims or offenders in the room. I did not see Mr. Door Kicker or Ms. Sob Lady.

That was nothing new to any of the officers present. Many times, after all our work, either the victim or the offender or both would not show up. The cases were then dropped. They were "stricken on leave to reinstate," or in some cases warrants were issued. Toward the end of the court call, Mr. Door Kicker and Ms. Sob Lady showed up arm in arm. They were both dressed in all white. They walked down the aisle like they were on *Soul Train*.

When I alerted the state attorney that they were in court, the case was called. Ms. Sob Lady asked that all the charges be dropped as she would not testify against Mr. Door Kicker. Now I wanted to pop her myself. And then, wait for it, she asked if the judge would marry them. At that point, the people who were left in the courtroom burst out laughing. After many resounding bangs of the judge's gavel, order was restored.

The judge politely informed Ms. Sob Lady that this was a criminal court, not a justice of the peace facility. Mr. Door Kicker and Ms. Sob Lady left the courtroom arm in arm. I thought to myself, "Homicide is probably in their foreseeable future." I hoped I would not be the one assigned. Case closed.

IT'S MY CHILD

We got a call to see a woman about a disturbance with her daughter. It was another brutally cold Chicago day—fifteen degrees with a twenty-mile-an-hour wind. The wind chill was minus two degrees. An added plus was that there was about five inches of snow on the ground. Altogether, a thoroughly unpleasant Chicago winter day.

We trudged up to the (guess which floor) third floor. If I were ever elected mayor I would permit no buildings higher than two floors. We knocked. The door was answered by a pleasant woman probably in her middle thirties. She explained the problem was with her daughter. Her daughter was fifteen years old. She had recently given birth to a baby girl.

To us, that was not all that unusual. Children having children was not uncommon where we worked. Fathers to those children were usually unknown or took no responsibility for the children. Usually, as soon as the girl announced she was pregnant, it was "Adios girl. I'll look you up again when I want "some." These so called "Baby's Daddy's" would go on to impregnate as many naïve teenage girls as would fall for their "I love you baby" bullshit.

Mom told us that the infant was only weeks old. Mom told us her daughter wanted to take the baby to see its father. The problem being that Baby's Daddy was a Southsider. Mom told us where she thought he lived. It was so far south that it was almost in Indiana. We were both Northsiders. We were not even sure Chicago went that far south. The daughter wanted to take the bus to see Baby's Daddy. We thought, in this weather, even if they had a car, which they did not, it would take more than an hour. She also would have to take multiple buses to get to Baby's Daddy's residence. Then at some point she would have to make the trip back. Mom told her she was not going anywhere with the infant in this weather. We agreed.

We turned our attention to the teen mother. My partner had a teen daughter. He took the lead in trying to talk to her about her responsibility as a new mother. The young girl was tall and thin. She calmly listened to my partner as he explained that taking an infant on such a long trip in the weather conditions we were experiencing would possibly endanger the infant's life. He also explained that waiting for the bus for even a half hour in this cold could compromise her health as well as the child's. Having reasoned with her, we awaited her decision to stay safely at home with mom and the baby. It was not to be.

Her response to our reasoned entreaties was "It's my child!". She told us she was going and taking the baby with her. We turned to mom. She was the legal guardian. We told mom if she did not think her daughter would obey her, we could take her in to speak with a youth officer. We told daughter that if she attempted to take the infant from the home she would be arrested for child endangerment. She told us we might as well arrest her now because when we left she was going to see Baby's Daddy with the baby. We could not arrest her for saying she would go, but we could take her in to see a youth officer with mom's permission. The Youth Officer could recommend counseling at one of the many agencies available to troubled youth. Our concern was not for mom or daughter but for the infant.

We told Daughter to get her hat and coat as she was coming with us. She vehemently declined our invite. We asked Mom to get Daughter's hat and coat. She offered the coat and hat to Daughter, who promptly threw them on the floor. Daughter's behavior was unacceptable. We informed her she was going whether she liked it or not. She impolitely informed us that she wasn't going anywhere with a couple "mutha-fuckin' cracker po-leese." Our feelings were hurt. We wanted everyone to like us. A tiny tear formed in the corner of my eye as we laid hands on Daughter.

Daughter morphed into a Tasmanian Devil. We wondered why a good and beneficent God would task his acolytes to wrestle with the spawn of the netherworld. But, tasked we were. Of course, we did not want to hurt Daughter, but she was making pain compliance a rising option on our list.

We finally got her on the floor with both hands restrained from flailing at us. We were sweating heavily because we were dressed in several layers of warm clothing. We decided to handcuff Daughter as we did not want to walk around with eye patches for the remainder of our careers. We tried again to reason with Daughter but all we got was "hate face." Her demeanor may be the reason that Baby's Daddy did not want to take the bus to see her.

We eventually got her up and out with a coat thrown over her shoulders. We put her in the backseat of our vehicle where she promptly slipped out of our cuffs. She banged them against the screen in our shield car. We were like, "What the fuck?"

When we got to the station lot, we had to re-cuff her. Her behavior had mitigated somewhat in that we did not wind up on the ground during the procedure. We brought her in and put her in the detention enclosure behind the front desk. It was generally used for juveniles whose parents were on the way to our police station. The parents would be with the young person while he or she was being processed by a youth officer.

While not under arrest, we did not think Daughter would sit and wait for mom and the youth officer. We told the desk mice what was up and then went to pick up Mom. Mom had a relative come over to watch the infant. We took Mom into the station. We called the youth department to let the officers know what was awaiting them in the station. They told us they would be a while as they had juvenile criminals to process first. We told Mom it would be some time before they came. She thanked us.

Did we help the situation? I do not know. We did, however, prevent the possible harm to an infant because of the whim of a teenage mother. Maybe she would learn from this. Maybe not. Someone once said that God cannot be everywhere; that is why he created police officers. What would you have done?

WELCOME TO THE NEIGHBORHOOD II

It was a beautiful fall day. I was on routine patrol when I saw a kid I knew. I stopped to chat. He had just graduated elementary school and was enrolled in a parochial high school. As we talked, I sensed a certain nervousness about him. I knew he had just had to put his dog to rest, and it seemed he was a little down in the dumps. As we talked a little more, I was surprised to learn he had been the victim of a robbery.

He related to me that "Mr. Street Robber" had approached him and said, "Break yourself, mutha-fucka." He did not know what the man meant. That made Mr. Street Robber angry. The kid was only thirteen years old. He was very afraid because the man made a move under his jacket, as if he had a gun. He gave the Mr. Street Robber his wallet. He had only four dollars. The man left and walked around the corner.

I asked if he had made a report. He told me he had not even told his mother because he was so afraid. I took him to his home and made a report. It was an armed robbery as a gun was implied. As I made the report, my victim told me he thought it was the guy who had just moved into the corner building down the block. I asked if he was sure. He said he was but I could tell he was still frightened.

After my report, I went to the building in question and checked the names on the mailboxes. I knew the name would be there; otherwise, how could the mail carrier deliver that government check? As I was in the lobby, an elderly resident walked in. I asked if someone new had just moved in. He told me yes and that he was going to complain to the landlord about the loud music from the apartment. I got the landlord's name and phone number from the resident.

I called the landlord and got the full name and date of birth for Mr. Street Robber. I learned he had moved in with his girlfriend and her ten-year-old child. I ran Mr. Street Robber for a photo and rapper. He had some priors, but this may have been his first robbery. I pulled up some identification records photos of other bad guys with similar photos. I went to my victim's home the next day for a photo lineup. Without hesitation, he picked out Mr. Street Robber. Now I had to collar Mr. Street Robber.

He lived in the third-floor apartment in the aforementioned corner building. Since it was still early, I hoped Mr. Street Robber was still enjoying his government-subsidized nap. I called for an assist, and a tactical team, responded. I walked to meet them in the alley, leaving my car in front of the victim's house. I asked them to take the rear stairway. I then went up the front stairway and knocked on each door, yelling loudly, "Gas man. We have a leak in the basement. Everyone must leave the building." Only one elderly man answered the door, and I quietly told him everything was OK.

When I got to Mr. Street Robber's door, he opened it for the Gas man and it were me. Surprise. My little subterfuge had worked. I placed him under arrest. His girlfriend and the ten-year-old were there. The ten-year-old was in a sleeping bag on the floor. The girlfriend started objecting to the arrest. I called the tactical team on the rear stairway and let them in the apartment. They took the shackled Mr. Street Robber into our incarceration way station.

I asked Mr. Street Robber's girlfriend why her son was not in school. She told me he had not been signed in at his new school since they had moved. He had not gotten his medical inoculation records yet, so he could not go to the new school until he did. Mr. Street Robber's girlfriend informed me what school he had attended prior to moving. I thought I might be able to help expedite his transfer to the new school instead of him lying on the floor in a sleeping bag all day.

I went down the block to have my victim's parents sign complaints. I told them I would notify them when I had a court date. I knew the state attorney would probably not go with an armed-robbery charge, but I would try. As I thought, the robbery was downgraded to a theft. Mr. Street Robber caught a break.

The next day, I went to the ten-year-old's school to see if I could help expedite the transfer to his new school. I was very surprised at what happened. I was buzzed into the school through a substantial steel door, where a security person was screening visitors, and then I was escorted to the school office.

After explaining why I was there and relating the name of the ten-year-old, a spontaneous celebration broke out among the teachers present. As other teachers came and went in the office, the joy was evident that the ten-year-old was transferring to another school. It was also evident that his mother being gone was an equal plus. It seemed that the ten-year-old was the equivalent of Damien the Antichrist. As they say, no good deed goes unpunished.

To top it all off, my victim and his parents never showed for court. They told me their son was still fearful of Mr. Street Robber and was afraid to testify against him—a lot of police work and resources down the crapper. The only consolation was that Mr.

Street Robber was eventually evicted for not paying his rent. The whole dysfunctional family moved on to cause chaos in some other section of the city. I was glad it was not mine.

I WANNA GO TO PRISON

When I first started foot patrol, I tried to get an idea of what problems I would face in the neighborhood to which I had been assigned. Some coppers who had a little more knowledge about the area filled me in. Until that time, I had been mostly concerned with black gangs and the violence between the gangs caused by the drug trade.

In the new area I was assigned to patrol, I was informed there was a white gang. Although the gang did not have much of a drug-selling market plan, they had a history of violence. I was also told that they wanted to kill a police officer. Yippee!

I was told that on some past occasion, the police were in pursuit of one of their fellow gang members for a weapons violation. During the foot pursuit, the gang member in question took to some railroad tracks to elude capture. Perhaps unknown to the gang member, there was a set of parallel tracks for a rapid-transit passenger train. Those tracks were electrified. In the gang member's haste to escape, he hit the electrified rail. Whoops. He died, of course.

The gang blamed his death on the police. Shame on the evil police for pursuing a gun-toting gang member. In retribution, the gang decided to kill a police officer. I was told it was probably just talk or *woofin'*, as it was called in the 'hood. I really did not want to be the one to find out if it was not *woofin'*. But the job is the job.

I made it my business to know all the gang members in the gang. I compiled quite a dossier on them. They knew that I knew who they were. I developed a system I called "identify-nullify." Basically, if I knew your name, gang name, address, date of birth, license plate number, girlfriend's name, etc., you were at a disadvantage. You could not commit a crime in my area without me having some idea who committed it and where I might find you. You could not duck me if you had a warrant or were behaving badly when I was not around. That info came from numerous street stops, searches, and field interviews.

I developed a reliable cadre of informants to report on goings-on when I was not on patrol. Most gang members are bullies and thieves. They usually wrong many people who dwell in their periphery. Those are the people who want them off the streets, out of the neighborhood, or locked up.

Sometimes an informant might be a jilted girlfriend or somebody the gang member had taken money from or beaten. There were many motives for why informants informed. It might even be a fellow gang member who wanted another member's girlfriend or to take that member's position in the gang. Whatever the reason, I was the beneficiary of all that information. Regarding informants, the only thing you must never do is burn an informant, no matter what. That could result in the informant's death. That is no joke.

As time went on, the gang's influence waned. The Spanish gangs were gaining influence. The white gang was a local bunch with no recruitment plan. As the members were jailed or left the gang behind, the Spanish gangs grew in influence. The Spanish gangs had a national organization and income from drug sales, and they were not averse to murdering rival gang members.

The white gang's pool of recruits shrank due to changing demographics. They made one last-ditch effort with some young teens initiated into the gang. One of the new recruits was the younger brother of one of the white gang's older members. I had talked to the older brother on occasion. The older brother, it seemed, saw the futility of where the gang life was leading him. Death or jail. Pick one.

The younger brother, however, seemed like he bought completely into the gang culture. Because he was the younger brother of a member, let us call him "Lil' Bro." Lil' Bro started graffiti-ing up the neighborhood with his new gang name. I caught up with him, and after a frank discussion, he agreed not to continue his "pissing-on-a-post" behavior. Not very long after, I caught him with some drugs. Because he was a juvenile (defined as sixteen or younger), the kiddy cops sent him home with Mom. That was not a good thing. Mom could not handle him.

Lil' Bro was arrested several more times for juvenile bullshit. Eventually he was sent to the Audy Home (juvenile detention). The Audy Home is a very dangerous place as it houses close to four hundred of the worst of Chicago's young criminals. I'm sure Mr. Arthur J. Audy, an advocate for exploited children and the first superintendent of the juvenile detention center, could never have envisioned his name being associated with the facility's current population. It was, however, good training for a juvenile's next step down into the whirlpool of incarceration, featuring the Cook County Jail and/or Stateville Prison.

One fine day, an informant told me Lil' Bro had obtained a firearm and shot at some rival gang members. The next time I saw him, a foot chase ensued. I caught him with a gun. He told me he was glad because he wanted to go to the prison. Bye-bye, Lil' Bro. Wish granted. I never saw him again.

HUH? WHO, ME? II

I t was close to five o'clock in the morning. My partner and I were getting ready to use our half-hour break to wolf down some breakfast. Shortly thereafter, we would hit checkoff roll call, then head home. It had been busy most of the night, but usually by five o'clock in the morning, even the criminal element was running out of gas. They were as tired as we were. Just as we were going to ask for "lunch" at five in the morning, we were given a job of disturbance in an alley. We acknowledged the assignment and started to head to the address given.

We came in low and slow with our lights off. When you watch TV, you see police cars with all their shit going. Sirens are blaring. Light bars are flashing. That is not the way to sneak up on wrongdoers. You do not take corners on two wheels, leaving a strip of rubber on the street. You do not slam doors while getting out of your vehicles. You do not carry five hundred jingling keys on you belt.

Coppers who are actually trying to catch the bad guys practice noise and light discipline. Are there circumstances in which having all your equipment activated might be appropriate? Yes. When life is in jeopardy. But even then, you may not want to let the bad guys know you are coming. Light travels at 186,000 miles per second. Sound travels one mile in five seconds. So, junior police aspirants, if the bad guys have a lookout, they will see you coming rather quickly if you look like the spaceship in *Close Encounters of the Third Kind*. They will also hear you slamming those doors when you pull up on a burglary. Giving the bad guys a heads-up to your arrival is not a good thing tactically.

As we pulled slowly into the alley, we saw no disturbance. We observed an auto parked behind an abandoned building. All we saw were the taillights. As we pulled up, two guys bolted from the vehicle and ran up the stairs of an adjacent building. I do not know if they thought they were ninjas and that some magic made them invisible to us, but we clearly saw them run up the back stairs of the building.

We called in the plate and gave our location. The plate came back as a steal. The two ninjas were up on the third-floor porch lying down. In whatever cuckoo land they were in, they thought we could not see them. We drew our anti-ninja pistols and started up the stairs. We did not know if the ninjas were armed, but we did not want to find out the hard way.

As we approached the third-floor landing, we observed that both of the invisible ninjas were pretending to not see us. We poked their invisible selves. They awoke and seemed surprised. They were pretending to be asleep at five thirty in the morning on the third-floor porch of a residence that was not their own. We told them to arise, and of course, we were subjected to the "Huh? Who, me?" response. The Bushido God would be ashamed that his ninjas failed to pull off the cloak-of-invisibility trick. More practice would be needed. We would give them a secure room in which to hone their ninja skill set. We cuffed the wayward ninjas.

They boldly claimed that they lived in the third-floor apartment. We knocked on the door of said apartment. The man who answered disavowed the criminal ninjas. Off we went to our simple Zen-like structure to process their disgraceful selves. Upon arrival, we searched the miscreants more thoroughly and put the contents of their pockets on one of our World War II government-surplus desks.

We notified the owner of the stolen car to meet us in the station to sign complaints on the unsuccessful auto thieves. The vehicle owner came to the station. During the process of signing complaints, he related that he had left some money in the car. I asked him the amount and if any of the bills had any markings or abnormalities. He described the money and markings. We checked the bills one of our arrestees had in his pocket. Bingo.

It was very distressing for us to see a ninja cry. We averted our eyes as we escorted them to our ninja-practice room. We said a fond sayonara and headed home to finally get some breakfast. Case closed.

THE BITE OF JOINT
MUSCLE JIMMY

I t was a busy night in the district. That was nothing new to the men of "Fort Forgotten" on the west side of Chicago. The calls came in nonstop. Most of the calls could be settled with some frank counseling. Many of the people we counseled had been guests in our system on previous occasions. They knew what to expect if our requests were disregarded. We had a suite of reflection rooms where one could reflect without outside interruptions or distractions (other than your current cellmate's snoring). It was a retreat for the common-sensibly challenged

Someone, though, was about to avail himself of our benevolence by volunteering to be our guest. A young man in his late twenties had imbibed too much alcohol, topped off with a snoot full of yayo. The mixture of alcohol and cocaine produced an irrational being who felt he was smarter and stronger than those around him. In this case, those around him were the police. His mother had called the police because he was knocking around his live-in girlfriend in their third-floor apartment. The third-floor assignments were God's way of keeping his blue-shirted acolytes in shape.

When we heard the call come out of a violent domestic disturbance, we figured we would tag along to challenge our stair-climbing abilities. Another car also pulled up to challenge us on the assist. The officers assigned to the call were already upstairs. Upon entry to the stairwell, we heard the loud talking typical of a drunken cocaine user. We all raced up the stairs. Our unit won the race by a hair. The other assist unit demanded a review of the tape.

Upon entry into the apartment we observed the assigned unit explaining to a drunken cocaine addled man that he was going to jail. He looked like Joint Muscle Jimmy. We found later that he had developed those muscles while an unwilling guest in one of our tax payer supported, guard towered health facilities. He was told he was going to jail for battering his girlfriend. It was explained that he could go easy or go hard. It would be his choice. He chose hard. It was a bad choice.

Why he wanted to challenge six police officers to take him into custody was baffling. He was on parole so he was no stranger to the system. This incident plus resisting arrest was probably going to send him back to his fitness buddies in the yard, buffing out for their same-sex man friends.

Joint Muscle Jimmy threw down the gauntlet. We accepted the challenge. The scrum was on. The fur ball lasted less than a minute, during which time Joint Muscle Jimmy bit one of the first responding unit's members. But, Joint Muscle Jimmy was not yet done. He would resist to the last. At the time, we did not know he was on parole, but he did. While being led down the stairs, he pulled away from the escorting officer to attempt escape. That did not work out well for Jimmy. After his initial steps, he lost his balance and fell down a flight of stairs. We rushed to help him, but after having failed once in his attempt to escape the long arm of the law, he tried once again with the same result.

Now suddenly he became more amenable to our helping hands as we guided him down the final flight of stairs without incident. We checked him for injuries. He seemed okay. His big muscles must have cushioned his falls. He even told us he felt fine. We were glad. He would need more practice on the prison "yard" balance beam.

Our comrade, however had to go to the hospital to be treated for a human bite. When we went to court on Joint Muscle Jimmy, our state attorney seemed more like his public defender. She would not charge him with battery to a police officer. She intimated to us that it was part of our job to get hurt during the arrest process. I wonder if she would have felt that way if she were sporting a bite-mark scar on her "beach body."

We argued with her to no avail. Thankfully, the judge was not of the same mind as our state attorney. He added some time to Joint Muscle Jimmy's parole violation. Perhaps when Jimmy got out, he could look up the state attorney and thank her for defending him. But, considering his behavior with his former girlfriend, I do not think that relationship would come to a satisfactory conclusion. Case closed.

OOPS! II

We were on a routine call in the Murder Building, if there was such a thing as a routine call in the Murder Building. As I explained in *Book One* the Chicago Tribune had dubbed it that, due to the amount of murders committed within and just outside its immediate environs. The building was inhabited by a goodly number of felons and parolees. It was a very dangerous and violent place.

To give you a flavor of what it was like, I will quote parts of the *Chicago Tribune* article from November 27, 1988, written by Anne Keegan, titled "'Murder building' devastates a city block."

"It is a structure feared by many of the roughest of the street-wise. Everyone knows it simply as 'the murder building.'

"'They call it "the murder building" because people have been known to go into that building and not come out,' said one young man standing on a nearby street. 'You got to stay away from that place. Things go on in those halls that you don't want to see.'

"This building is more than just a frightening place. It is a monument to the urban slum; a walk through is a visit to a Third World America."

There is much more to the article, but you get the gist of it. If you want to know more, use your search engine and read the whole article.

Having said all that, here we were. My partner and I were handling a domestic disturbance in the entrance hallway. We were listening to our complainant's story of unrequited love, when we heard footsteps behind us on the stairway to the second floor. I was concentrating on the man to my front while my partner had my back.

My partner turned to the stairway in time to see two men in their mid-thirties running quickly down the stairway. When the first guy hit the hallway and saw us blue-shirted law dogs, he tried to put it in reverse. The guy behind him ran into him. They both were trying to go up and down the stairway at the same time. My partner pulled his pistol and told the men to grab the wall.

The two desperados had succumbed to *Officer Murphy's "Flat Squirrel Theorem."* Almost everyone has seen a flattened squirrel in the roadway. The squirrel is flat because it was indecisive, as were the aforementioned desperados.

Now in Mayberry RFD with Sheriff Andy Taylor and his deputy, Barney Fife, no one would pull a gun on two men running quickly down a stairway. Hell, Andy did not even carry a firearm, and Barney had an unloaded revolver with a bullet in his shirt pocket, just in case. But, as explained, we were not in Mayberry. We were in a building that even by Chicago standards was just short of a North Korean gulag.

As instructed, the two "Flattened-Squirrel Gangstas" grabbed the wall. I told our original complainant we would return at a later time to sort through his pressing romantic problems. However, to the untrained ear, it might have sounded like, "Get the fuck out of the hallway." The acoustics in that building were terrible.

I covered my partner while he searched both men. As it turned out, the Flattened-Squirrel Gangstas were both high-ranking members of one of the predominant criminal street gangs in the area. Both men were armed.

After the first pistol was detected, both men were cuffed and underwent a more thorough search. That turned up a Smith & Wesson .38-caliber four-inch revolver and a Charter Arms .38-caliber two-inch "snubbie." The Smith & Wesson, it turned out, was taken in a burglary. Another "twofer." Yippee. The master criminals had run afoul of the blue-shirted beat cops of the city whose Native American name, "Shikaakwa," meant *bad smell*. With that as precedent, they could have named that building "Shikaakwa" as it was quite the olfactory delight. Into the hoosegow went the Flattened-Squirrel Gangstas. They would be hauled before the bar to face Lady Justice for their nonconformity to the rule of law.

Law Dogs – 2 - Flattened-Squirrel Gangstas – 0
Case closed.

STRAIGHT BOBBY'S
LAST BURGLARY

I n *Beat Cop, Chicago Blue, Book One,* I explained that two brothers and their family and friends were a nightmare of criminal activity. They had not subscribed to the old saw of "don't shit where you eat." If you do not adhere to this maxim, you may wind up mixing crap with your edibles.

In a practical sense, it means do no wrong where you work or live. Some recent national examples of violations are pretty-boy presidential candidate John Edwards and Governor Arnold Schwarzenegger. Both disregarded this common-sense saying and shat where they dined, and I would argue to no good end.

In the case of which I speak, a heroin addicted burglar was brought low after having violated this simple rule on multiple occasions. The first night after they moved in on my beat, the store-front thrift store in their building was burglarized. Operating cash was taken. On the second and subsequent nights four more commercial burglaries occurred. If you guessed that my two prime suspects were Straight Bobby and Curly Bill you are dead on.

The back door to their rat's-nest apartment provided egress to a space between their building and the next. In the space between the buildings was a stairway. The outside stairway led to second-floor apartments. Due to the proximity of the buildings to one another, the felonious duo had access to all the flat rooftops for almost an entire block. All they needed to gain access to the businesses was to cross the roofs, descend the stairways between buildings, and break into whatever door or window that allowed access. Most businesses did not have alarms. All the buildings had locked steel gates at the alley, preventing police access between the buildings.

To my knowledge, in my patch, they stuck to commercial nighttime burglaries. I heavily patrolled the alleys during the day, so daytime burglaries were not practical for them. On afternoons and evenings, people were home, so that was not practical either. During the day, it seemed, they did their dirt in the adjoining suburbs where they could be somewhat anonymous.

Fast-forward a couple years. While the residential burglaries in my patch were very low, some garage burglaries were on the rise. Residential burglaries normally take place during the day. Garage burglaries usually take place in the nighttime hours when most people are asleep. These are not hard-and-fast rules but represent a norm with few exceptions.

One fine night Straight Bobby got a tip that there were drugs and guns in a van parked inside a residential garage. The residents of the building were the brother and mother of a major gang leader. Neither the brother nor the mother of the gang leader were in any way associated with the gang's activity. Perhaps Straight Bobby's crack-addled, 'hood rat tipster said what he said to get another hit on Straight Bobby's crack pipe.

Straight Bobby, wearing a hooded sweatshirt, stalked down the alley to the garage in which he assumed a vanload of illicit goodies was hidden. He finessed the garage door by booting it, which woke the family dog. The dog's barking alerted the man who lived there. The man who lived there grabbed his mom's rolling pin from the kitchen counter and went out in his yard to see what his dog was barking at.

The man saw a figure in a hooded sweatshirt running from the side door of his garage. The victimized man launched the rolling pin at the hooded figure. The rolling pin hit Straight Bobby on the bean. The throw was a "ten" in the Olympics of rolling-pin throws.

Straight Bobby yelped in pain and grabbed his head where the rolling pin had hit him. By doing so, the hood on the sweatshirt fell away. The man recognized Straight Bobby from the neighborhood. Too bad for Straight Bobby. He scooted down the alley and made good his escape.

The next day while I was on patrol, Straight Bobby's victim flagged me down. He related to me what had happened. I made a report and then went on the hunt. The last time I had seen Straight Bobby, I had arrested him for mail theft.

What prompted that street stop was that I saw Straight Bobby walking down the street carrying a Time Life book. I asked Straight Bobby what he was doing with a brand-new Time Life book. He said he had found it on the sidewalk, and he was on his way to sell it. I retraced his steps and found the discarded cardboard mailer in a bush. I arrested Straight Bobby for mail theft, took him in, and notified the US Postal police.

That case went nowhere as the complainant did not wish to pursue it, and the Postal Police were on another case and could not send anyone out. It pained me, but I had to release Straight Bobby. On the plus side, I learned he was homeless and living in a city park. The landlord of the building in which he had lived had finally evicted the whole felonious family.

I asked a couple homeless men I knew about Straight Bobby. I had fronted these guys some cash for food on several occasions. Money well spent. They told me Straight Bobby was living in a bush with his whore girlfriend. I called for an assist. We beat the bushes around a fenced-in football field in a city park.

Straight Bobby and his girlfriend were so well hidden we almost did not find them. They had tunneled out a rudimentary living space in the bushes along the fence. His girlfriend must have been so proud of her man. I'll bet when she was a wee tot she never envisioned herself living in a fucking bush with a dope-addict thief. Straight Bobby caught seven years based on his tome like rapper.

There were several guys I kept track of when they went inside. Straight Bobby was near the top of my list. I used the Bureau of Prisons website to keep track of bad guys who were getting paroled back to my patch. Straight Bobby was paroled after two and a half years. I kept an eye out for him but did not see him. I called his parole officer. He told me Straight Bobby had failed to report to him. A warrant had been issued. The hunt was on again.

Again, some tipsters guided me to the general vicinity of Straight Bobby's new abode. He was living under a major expressway bridge. Under the bridge where the soil of the berm bordering a major cross street met the underside of the bridge, there were exposed steel girders. Between the girders was a space approximately five feet wide, four feet high, and about two feet deep. Across each of these seven to ten spaces, wires were attached and crude curtains were drawn over each space. I woke Straight Bobby from his new rat's-nest bed. I violated his parole. He went back to serve the remainder of his time. I never saw him again. Perhaps when he got out he set up housekeeping in an abandoned gopher hole. Case closed.

DON'T FUCK WITH THE TRUCK

We were working the south end of the district. We hadn't been assigned a call yet, so we were hitting the streets and alleys. I was with my assigned PPO. Most people who have never lived on the streets we patrolled don't realize the amount of criminal activity we confronted daily. You could barely go four blocks in any direction without running into a drug operation. That criminal activity alone would tax any police department. Add into the mix robberies, burglaries, auto thefts, and all sorts of disturbances, and you had a recipe for criminally caused chaos.

The drug operations had lookouts plus rabbits. Rabbits are designated runners who would bolt when you stopped to investigate illegal drug-related activity. The rabbits usually had no drugs or warrants. They were there to lead you down a rabbit hole. That took you away from the drug stash and the money man. The drugs would then be retrieved and moved from the area of your investigation.

The money man usually had no drugs on him. You could not just take his money unless you observed a hand-to-hand transaction. The stash man hid the drugs in any number of places limited only by one's imagination. The stash man would go to the stash to get the drugs after the money man gave a signal, usually a hand signal, indicating the quantity paid for. The hype customers then picked up the drugs from the stash man.

So, if you were in a blue and white, unless you had specific information on where the stash was and who was dispensing it, you could not really set up a surveillance. The dealers had lookouts and what they called security to watch out for police and gang rivals.

In a blue and white, you would be as obvious as a diamond in a goat's ass. If you did manage to grab them with the drugs, they would have a new crew on that corner within minutes of your departure. That kind of activity ran on an endless loop day after day, night after night.

Sometimes, if we sat on a drug corner long enough to inhibit the flow of nitwits coming to purchase their version of chemically induced euphoria, the dealers would have anonymous callers put in calls. They would call in a man with a gun or a robbery in progress. The phony calls would pull us off the corner as the assigned unit or as an assist car. It was a continual game of cat and mouse. They would adapt to our tactics, and we would adapt to their tactics ad infinitum.

Tactical units were on the streets as well. They were in unmarked cars and civilian clothing. They were a little harder to spot. But the unmarked cars were obvious also. They were usually one solid color with "M" (municipal license plates) and sometimes a spotlight. They weren't as easy to spot as a blue and white with a light bar but were still obvious to the criminally knowledgeable. The tac units did a great job of taking down some of the corners, but as I said, it was an endless loop. There were only temporary victories. We won tactical battles. Within the limits imposed on us, we would never win the war.

The drug business was demand driven. As long as there was a demand, there would be a supply. Also in the 'hood, there was a never-ending pool of uneducated, unemployable, young, nitwit gang members whose first and last job would be slinging drugs.

The other problem we faced were the drug users. As explained in other narratives, they needed the money to buy the drugs that the dope man sold. To get that money, the drug users committed every crime imaginable from shoplifting to murder. Their eagerness to alter their reality fueled a never-ending crime wave. So, as my PPO and I patrolled the streets and alleys, we knew it was just a matter of minutes before we observed wrongdoing or were tasked to respond to some criminal hijinks in progress.

The patrol function was all that prevented complete criminal anarchy. The victims of these thugs were glad to see us on patrol. In the 'hood, if you were brave enough to sit on your front porch, you might see a police car on your street as many as eight to ten times in a twenty-four-hour period. By performing the patrol function, we gave the legit citizens a break from the street thugs. It also gave us a heads-up of who was where when shit broke.

When you were on patrol in the wagon, you were pretty obvious to the bad guys. It was a one-ton rolling jail. Instead of playing cat and mouse with the bad guys, it was more like rhinoceros and mouse. The wagon was big and slow, but in an area of consistent traffic congestion, it really did not matter that much if it did not rocket from zero to sixty in six seconds. We were, however, about to be in a race, which we would win for a soon-to-be-evident fact.

We had just shown the flag down about five blocks of streets and alleys. There seemed to be nothing popping. We were about to swing through another alley to check for evildoers. As we made the turn, there sat a vehicle with two occupants, lights off, motor running. Not unusual, you might say. You would be right if the driver of the vehicle did not slam it in reverse and start backing down the alley a high rate of speed. Now here was a race the wagon could win. My PPO activated all of our bells and whistles. I'm not sure what that driver thought as I was about ten feet off his front bumper as he sped backward down the narrow alley. I think he might have thought, "Oh, fuck," but that is just a supposition on my part. Surprise. He crashed. How very sad. I think we made him nervous with our "shock-and-awe" light show.

We bailed out of the truck as the suspects tried to skate. They didn't make it. How tragic. On the plus side, though, in their haste to boogie, they forgot their gun. Boo hoo. There in plain sight on the front seat was a Smith & Wesson blue-steel, .38-caliber handgun. Gee, maybe we interrupted a crime about to happen.

We put the speedsters in the back of our truck and delivered them to "Lookin' Like a Clown with Your Pants on the Ground Snack Bar." PS They also got a traffic ticket for improper backing. Yippee. Case closed.

THE REPO MAN AND
THE SLED DOG

I t was a cloudy January day. We were working the third watch in a beat car that covered the far south and east sectors of our district. There were multiple factory buildings bordered by residential streets. I was working with a new guy who had just completed his training period. He was now the "real police." Little did I know I would be working with one of the best police officers in the department in my opinion.

We were cruising down a city street that divided the residential area from the industrial area. I was driving while my partner was looking out for evildoers. As a car passed in the opposite direction, my partner said, "Stop that car."

I swung a U-turn, and we turned on our version of the Super Bowl halftime show. The bad guys turned down a street between two factories. By doing that, they kind of screwed themselves. That street led to a T intersection with a one-way street at the end of it. There was almost no place to run and hide.

They pulled over. We called in our location and the plate number of the car. There were four of them. We got them out of the car and put them into the modified front-leaning rest position on the hood of their vehicle. Our plan was to search them, then search the car.

My partner was standing back monitoring the actions and movements of the individuals I was searching. I got lucky on shitbird number one. In his right front pocket, I found a .32-caliber semi-automatic hand gun. I said "gun."

With that, my partner put the other three bad guys in the extended front-leaning rest position. This position was a little less comfortable because the bad guys' mugs were flush against the hood of the car. I cuffed up dufus number one. My partner had drawn his weapon in case shitbirds number two through four had any further armament. They did not. They were transported, then processed and housed.

When I finally got a chance to talk to my partner, I asked how he knew those guys were dirty. He told me he looked at their eyes, and he could tell with near certainty that something was not right. Using the scientific method to prove or disprove a premise, a street stop was necessary to gather facts to support this conclusion. Hence, an evildoer's gun was taken off the street. Bottom line, the "Repo Man" was a hell of a cop.

He teamed up with a guy I nicknamed the "Sled Dog" because he looked like an Alaskan Malamute. The Sled Dog was also a good copper, but he was one those guys who had no filter on what he said. So, if the Sled Dog thought you were an idiot, you knew he thought that because he said it to your face. Most people will try to find a bullshit way to call you an asshole without saying the actual words. The Sled Dog had no such finesse. We always kidded the Sled Dog by saying he should open the "Sled Dog School of Manners and Etiquette."

When Repo Man and Sled Dog teamed up, they were a car-stealin', drug-sellin', gun-totin' criminal's worst nightmare. Almost every night they came in with a stolen-car, gun, or drug arrest. There was one twenty-eight-day stretch (a full police period of time) during which they came in with a stolen car every night. They were a great team. I called the Sled Dog's partner the Repo Man because of the stolen cars and car thieves he brought in. These two officers defined proactive policing. The city's taxpayers got their money's worth from that duo.

The Repo man eventually became a homicide detective. The Sled Dog became a sergeant. I enjoyed working with them. They were indeed the "real police."

DUCKIN' THE FUZZ

I was walkin' and stalkin' down the avenue. It was a fine July day, about midmorning, when I spied a wanted man coming in the opposite direction. One of the local 'hood rats who did not like this guy told me he had a burglary warrant. I already had all his info because he belonged to the resident street gang in my area. I did a computer check after roll call, and sure enough, the info was right on.

He was walking casually toward me when the realization hit him that I knew about his burglary warrant. He pulled his baseball cap down over his face and began walking away from me at a fast pace. He was about half a city block from me and was headed for the corner. Just before he turned the corner, he gave me an over-the-shoulder glance—a tell.

I was approaching the corner nearest me, a block from where he made the turn. I turned down the block and headed for the alley. He figured I would be running down the block after him, so he doubled back in my direction in the alley. When I turned into the alley, he was coming right at me looking over his shoulder.

Whoops. I started to trot toward him. When he saw me, he did a quick left into a perpendicular alley.

At the time, I was in my mid-fifties. He was nineteen. In the police game, you do not have the benefit of a handicapper to even the playing field regarding age and fitness. It is what it is: an old man chasing a teen.

I was in decent shape, so I loped after him with all my gear bouncing and jostling. I got on the radio and called in a foot pursuit for a man wanted on a burglary warrant. Help was on the way. He still had a little more than half a block head start on me. He used to live in the neighborhood where the pursuit was taking place, so he had sympathetic friends in the area. As it turned out, so did I. He turned the corner at the end of the alley. I wasn't sure if he was going to double back on me again. I lost sight of him.

When I reached the end of the alley, he was gone. Now here is where all my time at the local elementary school paid off. One of the young kids from the school asked if I was chasing a guy. I said yes. He pointed to where he had gone.

I ran two half-blocks, and another kid from the school pointed me down another alley. As I got halfway down the alley, another kid in a yard told me which yard my guy had ducked into. I was relaying information to the responding units as I ran. They had that street covered. I could not go into the yard because there was a dog in it. The dog gave me every indication that trespassing into his domain would not be permitted.

I was familiar with the house as it was the home of a gang sympathizer. The officers in front entered the building and found our guy in the basement hiding behind the furnace. He was unceremoniously yanked from his hiding place, and out the door he went guided by our helpful tactical officers.

I cut through another yard to the front of the building. Some of "Burglar Boy's" friends were in the street protesting his arrest. Guess what? We had room for them too. We had well-guarded protest rooms where they would be free to protest away, unless their cellmates wanted to take a nap. In that case, they would have to make a silent protest. They are the best kind when you are locked up with "Bubba the Bone Breaker." He likes his quiet time.

So, a big thanks goes out to the neighborhood junior police kids and the fast-responding men in blue. The violator of both the eighth commandment and the laws of the state was brought to the judicial process against his will. Case closed.

MOLESTER

In the state of Illinois, a person convicted of a sexual offense must register with the city he lives in after he is released from prison. That said, I was on foot patrol one fine day when I spotted an unfamiliar face. He had a baseball cap pulled down partially covering his face. He was leaning against the wall of a building where my resident burglars lived. I thought this fellow might be worth a chat. I ambled over to see if he was a new mope to add to my mope collection or if the building had a structural defect. Perhaps he, like the little Dutch boy with his finger in the dike, was preventing the tragic collapse of the building by leaning against it. Perhaps he would need my assistance.

My first assumption had been correct, in that when he ceased leaning against the wall of the building, it remained upright. Whew.

When I questioned him about his mopery it came to light that he was a registered sex offender. I inquired as to why he occupied his present location on my beat. He replied that he just wanted to rest and pick his teeth with the toothpick dangling from his mouth. His answer was unacceptable, and I told him to move along in a direction that would preclude him passing near the school on my beat. He did so.

The next day, I ran his info for a sheet and filed it in my mopery collection. He was up to date on his reporting, so there was no need to hassle him further, as long as he stood clear of the children on my beat. After that first encounter, I ran into him several more times, but he was breaking no law, so he just remained a small blip on my radar.

A few months passed, and as I patrolled my beat, a pre-teen I knew from the school flagged me down. She told me her mother wanted to talk to me. I went to their home, and the mother told her daughter to fill me in on what had happened.

It seems the girl's friend and another girl, both ten-year-olds, had met with "Mr. Molester" down by the railroad tracks behind a factory. After they met, one girl voluntarily began to fondle Mr. Molester's man parts. The other girl objected to this behavior and told her friend if she continued, she would leave and call the police. Both girls then left. One of the girls told the pre-teen who had summoned me, and she told her mother.

This incident took place just before she flagged me down. I put her and her mother in the back of my squad car to go look for this guy. I was pretty sure it was Mr. Molester who had been involved, but in our little slice of Chicago, there were more registered sex offenders than most people were aware of. I wanted to make sure I had the right guy. The young girl had seen him before and could ID him.

I went to the tracks where this had taken place and started looking from there. I figured if he walked down the tracks to the next major street, he would turn up near a football stadium on that street. Or, he could keep walking and wind up in a neighborhood where he would be unwelcome—a rough area where they might shove that ratty toothpick into his eyeball.

Just as I was making the turn, I spotted him. I asked the girl in the back if this was the guy. She answered in the affirmative. I ran up on him with the squad car as he was running across the street into a southern suburb. He didn't make it. I was out the door and on him like a bulldogger at a rodeo. His face kind of bounced off the hood of the car. Good thing he had discarded his toothpick.

He would have plenty of time to pick his teeth back with his friends in Stateville. Although, many of the convicts had children and were not all that friendly to child molesters. I called for a transport, but there were no cars available. The mother and the girl said they would walk home. After the transport, I had to track down the girl involved and her mother. I would not be going home myself for quite a while. I felt good, though, that I got this guy before he did any worse. I had to wash my hands about three hundred times, but it turned out to be a good day for the men in blue.

LONG-SLEEVED SHIRT

My partner and I got a call to meet some suburban coppers at an address in Chicago. When we got there, they told us that they had arrested some mope for fighting with his cousin during a domestic argument.

As they are taking him into their lockup, he told them that he knew where there was a dead body in Chicago—at the building where our meet was taking place.

We took the guy out of their car and immediately threw a set of cuffs on him. Fifty percent of the time, the person who notifies the police that a murder has been committed is the person who committed the crime. On the off chance, he should break free of our iron grip, we did not want him running down the block completely unencumbered in his felony flyers.

We went upstairs, and he led us to a door. He said he only had one key for the door. It had two locks. We searched him. "Guess what?" He had the other key in his pocket. What a surprise! He said that he had forgotten he had it. We said that we understood because we knew he would never lie to us.

We opened the door. There was a full-length mirror facing us as we walked in. In the mirror's reflection, we observed the body of a young woman lying nude on the bed. Normally this would not be such a bad thing. We would see her and she would see us, and we would all have a very good time. But you knew there was going to be a "but," didn't you? She was dead. Now we could not have a good time. We were angry at the person who did this.

She was lying at the bottom corner of the bed. She had what appeared to be the shank of a screwdriver sticking out of her forehead. Her face was battered, and she had the sleeve of a shirt sticking out of her mouth.

We rummaged around and found out that she was from a Scandinavian country. We saw her picture with her mother on the dresser. She was a real good-looking babe. Not so much anymore.

We turned to the mope and asked him what happened to cause this young lady to become deceased. He told us that his cousin picked him up to give him a ride to his girlfriend's apartment. When they get there, the cousin said that his girlfriend lived there too. So, they both went in and found out that it was the same apartment and the same girl. They decided that they must teach her a lesson. And so, they did.

As she was being beaten, she started to scream, so the mope told us that his cousin took off his shirt and stuffed it down her throat to keep her quiet. It did. At that point, the forcible ménage à trois became a ménage à deux. The suspect said his cousin grabbed something from the kitchen and stabbed her in the head to make sure she was dead. After that, he said his cousin had sex with her, then they took all her money and left.

He told us he went for the beating and the robbery but that he was no murderer. What a humanitarian. His benevolence brought us close to tears because he only beat and robbed the victim but did not murder her. Perhaps a Nobel committee would award him a medal for his restraint.

He told us the reason he was arrested by the suburban cops is that he and his cousin were fighting over who should pay for the cousin's shirt (the murder weapon). Amoebas have more brain power. "Poor Inga," I thought. She did not know about America.

PCP AND THE BAT-SHIT-CRAZY NAKED MAN

My partner and I were working a two-man car on midnights. We monitored a call of a disturbance with a violent naked man. We decided to take a ride. We had been on the job for a while, but what would explain our wanting to take a ride on a violent naked man? Perhaps we were as deranged as the man we were going to confront. Some of our comrades would not debate that representation of our demeanor.

"Maybe," we thought, "if we could sufficiently establish a relationship with the violent naked man, we could reason with him." Our dreams however, were dashed when we arrived to find a man who had driven his shaven head between the bars of a wrought-iron fence. Another plus was that he had muscles on top of his muscles, not to mention his nakedness. Reasoning, it seemed, would not be an option. Shucks and damn.

It had been extremely hot and humid. This was also a problem. The muscular, naked, drug-addled man was heavily perspiring. He looked to us to be as slippery as a greased eel. We did not wish to wrestle with "Mr. Slippery." Wrestling with a slippery naked man who was grunting, drooling, and snarling was never a desirable way to end a shift.

We devised a plan. We would cuff his legs, cuff his wrists, then pop him out of the fence. Thus encumbered, we thought, he most likely could not hurt us. That was the plan. It is said of mice and men that often their best-laid plans go awry. This would be no exception. Awry the plan would go.

The leg cuffs were ratcheted around both ankles. So far so good. We got one handcuff on him, and then the plan unraveled. He began to grunt and snarl as he tried to pull his head free. As we tried to get his other wrist shackled, he popped his sweaty, slippery head out from between the bars of the fence. He almost amputated both ears by doing so. Then he came after us. Yikes! We emptied two cans of pepper spray into his face. It just made him madder, but it also compromised his vision. So now we had a snarling, drooling, angry, naked man who was blinded by pepper spray. Yippee. Where was the department rodeo clown when you needed him?

Thank God his legs were cuffed. After a very unpleasant fur ball with Mr. Slippery, we managed to get the other handcuff on him. A wagon pulled up, and Mr. Slippery was transported to a hospital, but the hospital refused to take him because he was so bat-shit crazy. He was then ushered into his own private cubical in our steel-barred mental health/drug rehab facility.

The next day when he had recovered from his self-induced state of insanity, he told us that he had eaten an exploding chicken. I guess when you think about it, dining on an exploding chicken would in fact cause you to ram your head through a wrought-iron fence. They walk among us.

THE PYRRHIC VICTORY OF
THE SPIDER-EGG KILLER

A Pyrrhic victory refers to the battle of Heraclea in 280 BC during which King Pyrrhus of Epirus defeated the Roman Army. The victory was temporary in that King Pyrrhus lost his whole army by doing so. Pyrrhic victory in modern usage has come to mean winning with such high cost that it effectively could be deemed a loss. Keeping this in mind will give some meaning to the following story.

I was working a one-man car on the midnights. About midway through the shift, I was assigned to assist the ambulance at the sub shop. I thought, "Piece of cake." An assignment during which I could also dine and chug a Coke. When I arrived at the scene, I was greeted by the ambulance crew, who walked me over to a body that had been stabbed multiple times. Not quite the piece of cake I had imagined.

It appeared that this was a homicide, or so I thought. However, my cop brain had been conditioned to expect the unexpected.

The dead man stabbed multiple times was unexpected. What happened next was super unexpected.

As has been said many times, the drug PCP has numerous side effects, one of which is the feeling that there are bugs crawling under your skin. In this case, the bugs were spiders.

It seems "Mr. Dead Fellow" had ingested some PCP. Not long after, he felt spiders under his skin. Mr. Dead Fellow's solution to eradicate the spiders was to stab them with a flat-bladed screwdriver. As PCP is also a potent painkiller, Mr. Dead Fellow may not have felt the pain caused by stabbing himself. We can only speculate.

Mr. Dead Fellow then felt the need to enter the local sub shop, where he may have thought spider-killing physicians were available. He spied some local gang members, whom he may have thought were in the spider-killing physician's waiting room.

Not willing to wait to be seen, he chased the gang members around the sub shop until they fled the crazy motherfucker with the bloody screwdriver. Mr. Dead Fellow then mumbled to the sub shop staff that the spiders had laid eggs in his throat. He then proceeded to stab himself in the throat until he died. His throat looked like he had been attacked with a chain saw. He had won his battle with the evil spiders, but at what cost?

While documenting what had happened, no one who heard the story believed it. Even the medical examiner doubted what had played out. He was initially going to classify it as a homicide. However, the sub shop had a video recorder running. That video showed the whole incident. In the end, I had lost my appetite, but right about then, a cold brew sounded good. A word of advice: beer is a cheap and effective spider repellent, but it must be taken in multiple doses to achieve the maximum benefit.

THE SUDDEN EPIPHANY OF
MR. S. HOLE

I responded to a citywide call of man with a gun. It was daytime, it was hot, and I was working a one-woman car in one of the busiest districts in the city.

The area where the call came from had multiple drug corners. As I turned the corner, a man fitting the description bolted. I came to a screeching stop. I was out the door in pursuit while calling out my location and direction of flight.

The bad guy was running across an empty lot when a tac car pulled up at the other side of the lot. The tac guys bailed out to cut him off. Just then, I saw him toss something as he was running away from me. He kept running, but like a pack wolves, the tac guys cut him off and brought him down.

I went looking for what he had tossed. The lot was full of discarded junk. I assumed I was searching for a gun because the call and the description broadcast was for that very reason. After a quick search of the area, I found it. It was a 9 mm semi-auto pistol. It was determined later that it had one round in the pipe ready to roll.

The tac guys searched and cuffed the guy, and we headed for the station with one in custody and the firearm recovered. I met the tac guys in the station lot. We walked "Mr. S. Hole" through the station doors and headed for the stairway to the tac offices upstairs.

As we started to climb the stairs, Mr. S. Hole turned to me and said, "Bitch, I should have killed you when I had the chance."

Just then, he crumpled up. A tac guy caught him just before he fell to the ground. However, his head had bounced off the wall before he was rescued.

It seemed like Saint Paul on his way to Damascus when he was struck from his horse and blinded by the Lord. Mr. S. Hole was also struck by an unseen hand. Glory be. Perhaps the Lord did not like Mr. S. Hole threatening one of his earthbound female blue-shirted acolytes. Mr. S. Hole had been brought to the redemptive process. Praise Jesus. He was on parole, so he would have the time and opportunity to change his ungodly ways. Can I get an amen? Amen.

Like Mr. S. Hole, I too had an epiphany. It was my first realization that if given the chance, and if the tac guys had not responded so quickly, Mr. S. Hole would have tried to kill me. That was the moment all that shit became real. Thank you, Lord, for not letting him kill me.

VINDICATION

We received a call of take an auto theft report. We relocated to the address given. The victim was a kindly old grandmother. Her sixteen-year-old granddaughter had taken the car. She had her permit and could drive with another licensed driver, but she could not drive someone else's car without permission.

We knew this was going nowhere, but a report had to be made. Even before we got done with the report, Granddaughter came back with the car. We had not yet got a records division number for our report, so all that remained was to go up and clear unless Grandma wanted to have Granddaughter locked up. She did not.

Granddaughter seemed like a good kid except for this incident. We were not that busy yet, so I put on my juvenile counselor's hat. As we sat on Grandma's front porch, we talked a little. Granddaughter was sorry for what she had done. Grandma had raised her. Like so many kids in the 'hood, her grandma was the stable link in her family.

The granddaughter's mother was not allowed in Grandma's house as she was an addict. Pop was only a faded memory. All she had was Grandma. I asked Granddaughter to look around from our vantage point on the front stairs. It was a rough neighborhood with no shortage of felonious mopes walking about.

I told her she had a choice. She could drift through school until she was old enough to legally quit, which was age sixteen. Then she could hook up with one of the 'hood rat bangers. She could carry her love child for nine months while she commiserated with her other pregnant friends about Pampers and baby formula. She could apply for all sorts of government benefits for being a single mother. Every now and then, when she saw Romeo, she could shout out to her friends, "There goes my baby's daddy" as he waved from a car full of other loser nitwits.

Or, she could finish school, go to a community college, meet a guy with something on the ball in said college, then have a shot at a better life out of this neighborhood. A plus is that she could then take Grandma to a better place, they would live happily ever after. As I left, I told her, "Think about it." I had given that same talk to numerous others. Maybe the light went on. Maybe it did not.

Five or six years later, I was working days. I was the transport car for a burglary arrest. As I walked in with three prisoners handcuffed together, one of the desk mice told me I had a visitor. I saw a woman on the bench in the desk area. I did not know who she was. I asked another officer to watch the prisoners for a minute while I went to see my visitor.

I said, "Hello."

She said, "Don't you remember me?"

I replied that I did not.

She said, "I am the girl who took her grandmother's car for a joy ride."

I was trying to roll back my rusty old Rolodex to remember, but it was covered with the cobwebs of time. So, I said, "Why did you want to see me?" She said she wanted to let me know that she graduated from college.

I was at a loss for words. Just then, the guy I had asked to watch the prisoners was calling my name. I had to go. I mumbled something about how glad I was that she had done what she had done, but I had to go because of the prisoners. I thanked her for taking the time to come in to tell me. Looking back, if there is one thing I can point to with a sense of accomplishment in my police career, it would be that one instance. I hope she is still doing well.

THE FALLEN—HEROES ALL

During my career from February 1, 1982, to February 3, 2004, fifty-three of my brothers and sisters were killed. They were all ages, races, ethnicities, and genders. I knew several of them. They all gave their lives for the safety of strangers. These are fifty-three of the total of 529 killed since the death of constable James Quinn in 1853.

Please read their names. Their families are without them. Please do not forget them. Keep the living in your prayers as well. (Asterisks denote a memory in the next chapter.)

Officer Benjamin Perez, September 18, 2002
*Officer Donald J. Marquez, March 19, 2002
Sergeant Hector A. Silva, October 2, 2001
Officer Eric D. Lee, August 19, 2001
*Officer Brian T. Strouse, June 30, 2001
Sergeant Alane M. Stoffregen, June 2, 2000
Officer James Henry Camp, March 9, 1999
Officer John C. Knight, January 9, 1999

Officer Michael A. Ceriale, August 21, 1998
Officer Richard R. Schott, December 3, 1997
Officer Frank Balzono, November 14, 1997
*Officer Gregory I. Young, September 18, 1997
Officer David C. Evans, August 25, 1997
*Officer Dell Fountain, March 23, 1996
Officer James M. O'Connor, September 16, 1995
*Officer Daniel J. Doffyn, March 8, 1995
Officer Gerald L. Wright, August 7, 1993
Officer John J. Lyons, October 5, 1992
Officer Robert H. Perkins, March 7, 1992
Officer Jimmie L. Haynes, August 17, 1991
Officer Eddie N. Jones Jr., January 7, 1991
Officer Johnny L. Martin, June 28, 1990
Officer Raymond C. Kilroy, May 13, 1990
Officer Gregory A. Hauser, May 13, 1990
Officer Elijah Harris, November 16, 1989
Officer Bruce R. Niedoborski, August 18, 1989
Officer William J. Luce, August 14, 1989
Officer Irma C. Ruiz, September 22, 1988
Officer John W. Matthews, May 21, 1988
Officer Helen P. Cardwell, May 19, 1988
Officer Lee R. Seward, December 30, 1987
Officer Arthur O. Jackson, September 30, 1987
Officer Gregory R. Edwards, September 29, 1987
Officer William M. Morrison Jr., September 4, 1987
Officer Jay F. Brunkella, October 4, 1986
Sergeant-Richard Davenport Jr., August 4, 1986
Officer George T. Bryja, July 27, 1986
Officer Richard W. Clark, April 3, 1986
Detective Wayne G. King, July 12, 1985
Officer Martin P. Clarke, August 26, 1984
Officer Curtis R. Baker, June 2, 1984

Sergeant John J. Collins, February 7, 1984
Officer Dorelle C. Brandon, January 25, 1984
Officer Fred Eckles Jr., January 17, 1984
Officer Anthony L. Creed, Aug 30, 1983
Officer Wayne J. Klacza, June 28, 1983
Officer Larry J. Vincent, January 14, 1983
Sergeant Hamp T. Mcmikel Jr., November 20, 1982
Officer Martin E. Darcy Jr., September 27, 1982
Officer John F. Lynch, August 19, 1982
Officer William P. Fahey, February 10, 1982
Officer Richard J. O'Brien, February 9, 1982
Officer James E. Doyle, February 5, 1982

MEMORIES OF THE FALLEN

D ONALD J. MARQUEZ—Officer Donald Joseph Marquez was shot and killed as he was serving court papers at the Logan Square apartments.

A seventy-seven-year-old resident opened fire with two .22-caliber handguns. Officer Marquez was struck several times. He succumbed to his wounds at the hospital. The assailant was shot and killed in an exchange of gunfire with back-up officers. Officer Marquez was a twenty-year veteran of the Chicago Police Department. He is survived by his wife, two sons, three daughters, one grandson, parents, two sisters, and three brothers.

Don was my classmate in the academy. He was so funny and quick witted that when you were with him, you never stopped laughing. He was an all-around good guy. After the academy, we would run into each other every once in a while. He always left you with a smile on your face.

The night he was killed, I was conducting an inventory of stolen merchandise from a secondhand store. Because of the volume of merchandise, two officers had been assigned to help me. We all heard the call of an officer shot in another district. The officers helping me wanted to go. I told them that there would probably not be much they could do that was not already being done. Sometimes if you are not essential to the situation, you just get in the way. Both officers were new to the job, and they wanted to help. I told them to go ahead. I did not know the officer shot was my classmate Don until the next day.

At first, I could not believe it. Marquez was a somewhat common name. I thought maybe it could be another Don Marquez. I just could not believe it was him. I thought God would not let that happen. It still hurts my heart even now. Sleep well, brother. You will never be forgotten. Save me a spot.

BRIAN T. STROUSE—Officer Brian Strouse of the Monroe District was shot and killed while conducting a surveillance of gang activity near West Eighteenth Place and South Loomis.

Officer Strouse was working as a plainclothes tactical officer. At approximately 2:00 a.m., he went into an alley, and shots began to ring out. Strouse, who was wearing a bulletproof vest and a police star on his utility belt, yelled out, "Police, drop your gun." Five more shots were fired.

A fatal bullet struck Officer Strouse. The other two officers ran toward the sound of the gunfire. They found Officer Strouse on the ground. He had been shot once in the chest and once in the head. His bulletproof vest had stopped the bullet to his chest. Officer Strouse was transported to a local hospital, where he succumbed to his wound seven hours later. On September 17, 2003, the gunman was convicted of first-degree murder. He was sentenced to life in prison.

Officer Strouse was a six-year veteran of the Chicago Police Department. During his career, he received sixty-one honorable mentions and a life-saving award. He was survived by his parents and three sisters. One of his sisters is a Chicago Police Officer.

I met Brian's sister Kathy before I met him. Kathy was a typical Chicago girl. She was tough. She was nobody's fool and was a good cop. Brian followed in her footsteps. Even though we did not know each other well, Brian and I would nod and say hi whenever we saw each other.

Brian was pretty intense from what I saw. He wanted to do the job. He wanted to get out there and stop the bad guys from hurting the good guys. He was reassigned to a different district where he quickly got on the tactical team. Just the fact that he had sixty-one honorable mentions lets you know he was out there working. Some officers do not get that many honorable mentions in a career, let alone in six years.

I ran into Kathy at a function recently. Her sadness over his loss was still in her eyes. Understandably so. God bless you, Brian. Sleep well, brother.

GREGORY I. YOUNG—Officer Gregory I. Young was shot and killed during a robbery attempt.

Officer Young was seated in his car when he was approached by two assailants who attempted to rob him. He identified himself as a police officer and was then engaged in a gunfight. He was able to wound one of the attackers before being fatally wounded. The second gunman was later taken into custody.

Officer Young's killer was convicted and sentenced to death. On January 10, 2003, George Ryan, the governor at the time, shamefully commuted the killer's sentence along with 164 other inmates on death row to life in prison. This was disgraced Governor Ryan's last act as governor before he went to prison. (A little street cred for when the governor would be joining his new friends in the clink. Maybe he could meet Greg's killer and shake hands.)

Officer Young was survived by his wife, daughter, son, parents, four sisters, and three brothers. His daughter followed in her father's footsteps and became a Chicago police officer.

Greg Young was a policeman's policeman. He was on my watch. He was a great guy. He had a booming voice, and his laughter made you laugh. His uniform was always perfect. You could cut yourself on the creases in his pants. I never saw him in a bad mood. His smile was always bright and sincere. For a while, I was the foot patrol on the beat Greg covered. You did not ever have to ask Greg for a favor; he would volunteer to help anyone who needed it.

One day I got some information that some gang members were using an abandoned house to smoke up. The only way in there was through a rear porch window. Then there was another window to enter the kitchen. I went to check it out. I got through the porch window, but I needed a boost to get through the second window. I called for an assist, and Greg volunteered. Now mind you, Greg looked like a police recruiting poster. Without hesitation, he came through the first window. When I asked for a boost, he smiled and said, "Nah, I'll do it."

Gregg was in terrific shape. He went through the second window like an Olympic athlete on a pommel horse. He opened the kitchen door. We went through the house together. It was full of gang graffiti and other evidence that gang members were using it as a meeting place. We secured it as best we could and called for the city to board the place up. This is just one example of his character.

Greg went on to the tactical team. He and a good friend teamed up. One morning when I came to work, I saw a female officer crying in the parking lot. I asked what was wrong. She told me Greg had been shot. He was dead. I could not believe it—he was such a life force. His partner was devastated as they were very close.

To this day, whenever I think of Officer Gregory I. Young, I remember his bright smile. What a great guy. I am sure his daughter will be just as good a police officer as he was. I miss you, brother. God bless you. Sleep well, brother.

DELL FOUNTAIN—Officer Dell Fountain was alerted to a disturbance in an upstairs apartment. The apartment was being used for narcotics activity. During the investigation, Officer Fountain got into a struggle with a man and was shot in the leg. The bullet severed a major artery. Officer Fountain died at the hospital from blood loss.

I did not know Dell very well. He was still new to the job and to our district. He seemed to me to be a serious person. People do not become police officers to sit back and watch the world go by. Officer Dell Fountain could have done nothing about the drug activity in the building where he was shot. Most of the people around Dell just let it be because they were afraid. Usually they are afraid with good reason.

Dell took his job seriously. He confronted the person involved with the suspected narcotics activity. A struggle ensued, and Dell was mortally wounded. What he did took courage. He had no one with him. He had no backup. In trying to stop drug activity in the building, he lost his life. His sacrifice was a testament to his courage. God bless you. Sleep well, brother.

DANIEL J. DOFFYN—Officer Daniel J, Doffyn was killed when he surprised burglary suspects at an apartment building. Daniel Doffyn and Mike Bubalo were new to the department and the district. After the afternoon watch roll call, they were going to their cars. They heard a call of a burglary in progress.

The call was across the street from the police station. They started to go toward that location. They were not assigned to the call; they just went. Meanwhile, Officer Elois Harrington monitored that same call. She headed for the apartment building as well. What all these officers did not know was that these three offenders had just fled the scene of a prior shooting. They went to the apartment building to hide. When they found no one home at their "safe house," they broke in.

A neighbor from the building reported the break in as a burglary in progress. Officer Harrington went to the opposite side of the building from Officers Doffyn and Bubalo. Officer Harrington confronted two of the offenders. She pointed her weapon at them and ordered them to get on the ground. One offender obeyed her. He was taken into custody. The other offender, who was holding a gun, fled around the corner of the building. Then, as Officer Harrington held the one offender at gunpoint, she heard numerous gunshots around the corner.

Officers Doffyn and Bubalo had gone to the front door of the apartment to investigate the burglary. Upon knocking at the door, they heard breaking glass then footsteps toward the rear of the apartment. Both officers ran to the rear of the building. Officer Doffyn rounded the corner. He grabbed one of the offenders, who began struggling with him. Officer Bubalo came around the corner and heard multiple gunshots. He saw Officer Doffyn and the offender he was struggling with fall to the ground. Officer Bubalo then observed the shooter holding and firing a Tec 9 pistol. The shooter had first fired the gun at Officer Doffyn then at Officer Bubalo.

A bullet struck Officer Bubalo in the left hip. The offender ran toward Officer Bubalo. Officer Bubalo returned fire. The offender went down. Officer Bubalo crawled to him and handcuffed him. Weapons, drugs, and money were recovered from the apartment the offenders had fled. They were all charged according to their crimes. Officer Doffyn was dead of two gunshot wounds. I understand Officer Bubalo had to have a hip replaced due to a gunshot wound that shattered the bone.

I knew Dan Doffyn just to say hello. He and Mike Bubalo were both tall with athletic builds. They were just the type of guys we needed out there. Once as we were walking out into the station lot, there was a strong-arm robbery at the gas station across the street from the district. Mike and I saw the offender flee, and we chased him. Mike passed me like a jet passing a bicycle. The offender in that incident had on his felony flyers. He beat both of us when he turned on the afterburners, then disappeared.

We don't win them all, but we try. I believe that it was Mike Bubalo's first day at the district. Welcome to the West Side. It seemed to me that when you saw Mike, you saw Dan. They were both good guys. They were eager to do the job they had trained for. They did so with honor.

Officer Elois Harrington, whom I knew as Elois Jackson, was a really nice person. She had a wonderful, bright smile. She was also very courageous. She had confronted two of the offenders, captured one, and caused the armed offender to flee. I think that day changed Elois and Mike. Seeing one of your own gunned down stays with you.

God bless you, Mike and Elois. Both of their lives would be forever changed. God bless you, Dan Doffyn. Sleep well, brother. I understand Dan's daughter Brittany wanted to become a police officer. She was eight years old when I saw her last. God bless. Stay safe.

REFLECTIONS

When working a beat car in a high-crime district, it sometimes seems like you are Sisyphus with his boulder. In Greek mythology, it is a boulder that Sisyphus must roll uphill for an eternity. In modern times, a *Sisyphean task* has come to mean a job that is laborious and futile.

After a while as a police officer, you slowly burn out. To some it is the end of patience in dealing with the daily ration of criminal behavior. It may also mean the loss of any human compassion or kindness for the victimized.

Like Sisyphus, your job seems laborious, futile, and totally without reward. You show up to work to try and get through another day. The brutally inhumane behavior of evil human beings is soul crushing. The prism you look through increasingly seems to reveal human beings at their worst with few exceptions.

What may give you some pleasure is legally depriving the bad guys of their freedom and then sending them to a place where they may be victimized. Putting away the bad guys, though, is not quantifiable in one important way. No one can say how many criminal acts were prevented by getting a criminal off the street. Since it cannot be measured, it goes unappreciated except among the brotherhood. Your fellow officers know what it means, but most citizens do not. Your hard work many times seems unappreciated by the very people you serve.

For some officers, the loss of empathy and compassion changes them not only on the job but in their private lives as well. It seems to them that most do not understand the inhumane deeds they witness daily. It seems that only other officers get it. That is a reality. This lack of understanding and unrealistic expectations by others sometimes causes walls to go up. Therefore, some officers feel that if you don't understand what I do or why I do it, you are against me. That becomes a reason to justify withdrawal from family, friends, or both.

In most cases, an understanding spouse or recognition that problems may exist, be they physical or mental, leads to an epiphany and correction of any self-destructive behavior. Sometimes that does not happen, and an individual is lost to whatever coping mechanism he or she uses to numb their physical or mental pain. That is a tragedy. When a job reshapes someone for the worst and they are lost to us, it is indeed tragic. Fortunately, most officers overcome whatever setbacks that are job related and go on to live long happy lives.

Many people who know police officers before and after they start the job say they notice a change in their thinking and behavior. Usually these people, when presented with the unfiltered truth rather than the cleaned-up version, are shocked. Most people would rather believe in the inherent nobility of man.

All that said, we do not pass the laws; we enforce them. It is the legislators who are elected who propose and pass these laws. They do so at your behest. Our task is enforcement. We may or may not agree with some laws, but when we put on the uniform and start our eight-hour tour, what we like or do not like becomes irrelevant.

Police officers perform heroic acts daily. They save lives. In some cases, they may lose their own lives by doing so. That is the one thing police officers are not tasked to do —they are not tasked to die for you. If they make the decision to preserve your life at the risk of their own, it is a sign not only of their heroism but of their character.

In my time on the police force, I have witnessed many selfless acts of heroism that go unreported and unrecognized. I have also witnessed extraordinary acts of human kindness that no one will ever know, with the exception of their comrades. The definition of integrity is doing the right thing when no one is watching. That is also the definition of a good cop. God bless the men and women who suit up every day to keep us all safe. Blessed are the peacemakers.

⊷⊶

Will there be a book three? I do not know. If enough police officers still have stories to tell, maybe so. I hope it happens, but if not, thanks for taking a ride with us. I hope my book left you with some understanding of what we street-grunt beat cops do every day. Thanks for taking the time to read about us. God bless you and the workin' police.